The Everyday Fish Cookbook

Simple, delicious recipes for cooking fish

TRISH DAVIES

SPRING HILL

Many thanks to all my friends and family for helping me with this book, especially Anna, Claire, Sarah-Jayne Hart and Lianne Bullard who tried and tested these recipes

Published by Spring Hill, an imprint of How To Books Ltd
Spring Hill House, Spring Hill Road
Begbroke, Oxford OX5 1RX
United Kingdom
Tel: (01865) 375794
Fax: (01865) 379162
info@howtobooks.co.uk
www.howtobooks.co.uk

First published 2012

How To Books greatly reduce the carbon footprint of their books by sourcing their typesetting and printing in the UK.

British Library Cataloguing in Publication Data
A catalogue record for this book is available from the British Library

ISBN: 978 1 905862 73 3

Illustrations by Firecatcher
Edited by Wendy Hobson
Produced for How To Books by Deer Park Productions, Tavistock, Devon
Typeset by PDQ Typesetting Ltd, Newcastle-under-Lyme, Staffordshire
Printed and bound in Great Britain by Bell & Bain Ltd, Glasgow

NOTE: The material contained in this book is set out in good faith for general guidance and no liability can be accepted for loss or expense incurred as a result of relying in particular circumstances on statements made in the book. Laws and regulations are complex and liable to change, and readers should check the current position with the relevant authorities before making personal arrangements.

Contents

3 Cold Lunches and Suppers   47

4 Hot Lunches and Suppers   60

Notes and Conversion Charts

In the recipes, eggs, and vegetables like onions, courgettes or aubergine are all medium-sized unless otherwise stated. Peel garlic and onions before chopping.

All the fish should be gutted and cleaned before you begin.

Wash and peel fruit and vegetables, if necessary, before preparing them for the recipe.

This book provides metric measurements, but those who prefer Imperial, or who want to use American cups, can use these conversions.

Weight

Metric	Imperial	US 100g = 1 cup	US 175g = 1 cup	US 225g = 1 cup
		Flour, nuts, breadcrumbs, etc.	Dried fruit, lentils, etc.	Butter, sugar, cream cheese, etc.
25g	1oz	¼ cup		⅛ cup
50g	2oz	½ cup		¼ cup
75g	3oz	⅔ cup	½ cup	⅓ cup
100g	4oz	1 cup		½ cup
150g	5oz	1¼ cups		⅔ cup
175g	6oz	1½ cups	1 cup	¾ cup
200g	7oz	1¾ cups		Scant 1 cup
225g	8oz	2 cups		1 cup
250g	9oz	2½ cups	1½ cups	1⅛ cups
300g	10oz	2¾ cups		1⅓ cups
350g	12oz	3 cups	2 cups	1½ cups
400g	14oz	3½ cups		1⅔ cups
450g	1lb	4 cups	2⅓ cups	2 cups

Weight

Metric	Imperial
5ml	1 tsp
15ml	1 tbsp
50ml	2fl oz
75ml	3fl oz
100ml	4fl oz
150ml	5fl oz
200ml	7fl oz
250ml	10fl oz
300ml	½pt
350ml	12fl oz
400ml	¾pt
600ml	1pt

Oven temperatures

Metric	Imperial
110°C	225°F
120°C	250°F
140°C	275°F
150°C	300°F
160°C	325°F
180°C	350°F
190°C	375°F
200°C	400°F
220°C	425°F
230°C	450°F
240°C	475°F

Measurements

Metric	Imperial
5cm	2in
10cm	4in
13cm	5in
15cm	6in
18cm	7in
20cm	8in
25cm	10in
30cm	12in

Foreword by Jean-Christophe Novelli

I have known Trish for many years as she teaches a seafood course at my cookery academy that is always full of people wanting to know how to cook, so I was honoured when she asked me to write a foreword to her book.

Trish was born in Sussex and learnt how to cook from her mother even before she had any formal training. Living by the sea, she naturally enjoyed lots of wonderful fish like sand dabs, cod, mackerel, crabs and brown shrimps, and she used to go along with her mother to collect the fish straight from the beach and only a few hours old. The local fishermen used to show them how to prepare the fish quickly and gave advice on how to store and cook the fish. Every four weeks, Trish and her mum used to prepare all sorts of fish for the freezer for friends and family. Even now she is very skilful and quick when preparing fish and a dab hand with a filleting knife.

Trish has written a number of cookery books and I found this one to be packed full of interesting, creative recipes that are not complex to make, so even a beginner will feel confident enough to try the delicious dishes. Preparing fish and shellfish is not difficult as long as you follow Trish's advice. The recipes also make use of basic storecupboard ingredients and only use the minimum number of ingredients, making them really simple to make. This book has well over hundred mouth-watering recipes and is packed full of tips and advice for anyone from beginner to well-qualified cook.

Trish also encourages people to eat more fish as part of a healthy diet. Fish and seafood are first-class sources of protein and provide many essential vitamins and minerals; oily fish also have the added benefit of containing omega 3 and are believed to promote a healthy heart.

In the book, Trish also talks about sustainability of fish stocks around the world and explains how important it is to buy eco-friendly fish: fish that is caught in such a way as to have no harmful effect on the stock, the marine environment or other species. That way we can enjoy all the benefits without depleting the fish stocks or damaging the environment. This book tells you how and what to look for when buying fish so you know you are buying responsibly.

This book is truly inspiring and will certainly be on my book shelf. I would recommend this book to any cook, from student to more experienced chef.

Bon appétit!

Jean-Christophe

Introduction

Fish is a wonderful food: delicious, healthy and offering us a huge variety of textures and flavours.

In Britain, we are lucky to be surrounded by seas that provide us with hundreds of different species of fish that we can enjoy as whole fish, cutlets, steaks and fillets. And that's not even starting on the fantastic range of shellfish and other seafood that grace our tables. Not only a valuable source of protein, fish also provides us with minerals. omega 3 and vitamins – it's certainly an all-round superfood.

Inspired by the variety of flavours on offer, this book provides you with a whole raft of ways to enjoy fish – not just on special occasions but every day. And since it is recommended that we eat at least two or three portions of fish each week, you'll find plenty of interesting opportunities you'll want to try. The recipes are simple to follow, demand no special skills, fancy equipment or expensive ingredients. You just need your usual kitchen equipment and the ingredients from your local fish counter or supermarket.

First, we'll give you some straightforward information on how to buy, store, prepare and cook fish so you learn the basic skills necessary to make the best of your fish cooking.

Types of Fish

Fish is classified into three main groups: white fish, oily fish and shellfish.

There are two types of white fish. The first is the round fish, such as cod, haddock, whiting, pollock, sea bass, coley and hoki, just to name a few. The second type is the flat fish, such as halibut, plaice, sole, lemon sole, skate, flounder and turbot. White fish has a more delicate flavour than oily fish and contains less than 2–3 per cent fat. It is light, nourishing and easy to digest, making it ideal for people on diets, old people and children (but that's no reason to save it just for them!).

Oily fish includes trout, mackerel and herring. It generally has a darker, richer slightly firmer flesh, which contains 10–20 per cent fat with about 80–160 calories per 100g. The fat contained in oily fish is mainly polyunsaturated, which is believed to help the functions of the brain and help to prevent heart disease. Oily fish are a good source of vitamins A, D and K, as well as omega 3 fatty acids – all essential in our diet.

Some fish are designated organic by the Soil Association, and this applies to farmed and controlled fish and seafood in the UK, covering a range of fish including trout and salmon.

As well as the old favourites, from prawns to haddock, the recipes include some of the more unusual species that have only relatively recently become available on our fish counters – fish like pollock and coley. These are now being sustainably farmed so are not only great for the environment, they are available at reasonable prices – and have some fantastic flavours. Try experimenting with them in place of the more familiar ones. You will find that some fish are available all the year round whilst those caught in inland waters in the UK have a closed season between 15 March and 15 June when the fish can't be caught, generally when they are breeding, so they are only available at certain times.

Sustainable Sources

The impact of overfishing on fish stocks and on the wider marine environment – fuelled by commercialism and by increasing demands for fish as the world population increases – is an issue of growing global concern. Other factors, such as climate change, are also contributing to the reduction of our fish stocks.

Always try to buy fish from sustainable sources: fish caught in such a way as to have no harmful effect on the stock, the marine environment or other species. By choosing such sources, consumers can help drive the market for sustainably produced seafood and make a real difference to the way our fish stocks are managed.

Farming is often suggested as the solution to the rising demand for fish. In the 1970s, cod and herring were overfished to such an extent that those caught were poor in quality. One solution was to farm fish to produce more, high-quality fish without further environmental damage. In Britain, mussels, lobsters, oysters and baby queen scallops are all produced in farms. Many seafood species, like warm water prawns, are farmed in countries like Thailand and Jamaica. The standards implemented by such farms have also come under scrutiny by the environmental lobby. However, the organic farming practices meet a high environmental standard, feeding stock with sustainably sourced foods, reducing the number of fish in cages, and including strict rules on the use of medicines, chemicals or treatment for parasites, such as sea lice on salmon.

Look out for the logo of the Marine Conservation Society (MCS) on the fish you buy. This is a charity that monitors these issues in the UK. It is a charity dedicated to the protection of British seas, shores and the wildlife that depends on them. The organisation also campaigns for clean seas and beaches, sustainable fisheries, the protection of marine life and their habitats and the sensitive use of our marine resources for future generations. One particular species of note here is the scallop. Sadly, as a response to high demand, dredging the sea beds for scallops has done so much damage off the British coasts that stocks will take a very long time to recover. Although you will pay a little more, it is therefore ideal if you can ask for scallops that have been collected by hand in order to ensure the long-term security of the marine habitats around the British coast.

Buying Fish

Buy from a reputable fishmonger or from an ice-chilled supermarket counter. The fish should be displayed on refrigerated counters or laid on well-packed ice. Note the standard of cleanliness and the way in which the fish is handled. The shop, supermarket or fish stall should smell fresh with no smelly 'fish' odour.

All fresh fish should look moist and undamaged. Look for fresh whole fish that have a firm, shiny body with close-fitting scales, clear, bulging eyes and bright pink or red gills. The body of the fish should be firm and springy to the touch and the bones embedded firmly into the flesh. Reject any fish showing signs of dryness or discolouration, or any that smell of ammonia or in any way unpleasant.

Cuts of fish – like fillets or steaks – should be firm and look moist. Fresh tuna should look pink in colour and not brownish; this often means it has been stored directly in contact with ice or at the incorrect temperature. White fish should be a good white in colour, salmon or salmon trout flesh should be bright red, trout should be pinkish.

Any live seafood – like crab, lobsters, langoustine or eels – should look lively. Crabs and lobsters sometimes have bands put on to their main claws to prevent damage to other lobsters in the tank. Live mussels, clams, oysters or razor shells should look bright, with the shells shut. Other seafood or shellfish should be bright and moist, not pale, dry or smelly.

Never be afraid to ask if the fish has been frozen or when it was caught; a good fishmonger will have all the details you want. If you wish to freeze the fish, make sure that it has not already been frozen. Most fishmongers label fish that has been previously frozen, but do ask if you are not sure. Some fish are frozen out at sea, then thawed at the dockside. This is fine if you are cooking immediately but not if you want to freeze the fish.

Make sure any frozen fish you buy feels frozen hard with no signs of partial thawing or damaged packaging.

The fishmonger will always prepare the fish for you if you are not too sure what to do, so strike up a conversation – you will find there is a wealth of knowledge there to tap into.

Storing Fish

Get your purchase home as soon as possible ideally in an insulated bag. When you get the fish home, store it carefully and eat it by the sell-by date.

Store fresh fish loosely wrapped in the fridge and cook within 24 hours of purchase.

Store shellfish in the packaging it comes in from the fishmonger; do not put it into a bowl of cold water or sealed container. Store in the base of the fridge at a temperature of 1–4°C and use within 12 hours.

Chill smoked fish, potted shrimps or marinated seafood as soon as you get it home and eat within 2–3 days or by the sell-by date.

Store fresh, frozen fish in its original wrapping at –18°C in the freezer for up to 2 months for oily fish or 3 months for white fish.

Cooked fish dishes that you have prepared and frozen keep for up to 2 months.

Thawing Fish

Fish frozen in breadcrumbs or batter do not need to be defrosted but should be cooked from frozen to make sure that the coating stays crisp and golden brown in colour.

Otherwise, thaw fish in its wrapping in the fridge until it is just pliable enough to handle, allowing about 6–8 hours per 450g of fish. Then drain it well, pat dry on kitchen paper and use immediately. You can defrost in the microwave but do so only in short bursts on the defrost setting otherwise you will cook the thinner parts of the fish.

Preparing and Cleaning Fish

Fish is usually sold cleaned and ready for cooking, either as whole fish or cut into steaks or fillets. If not, ask the fishmonger to prepare the fish for you and watch how it is done. If the fishmonger is busy, arrange to collect your purchases later when you have done the rest of your shopping. If it is not prepared, you'll need to go through the following steps.

Gutting a Fish

Have a large clean surface ready to gut the fish, which you should do as soon as possible. Lay a couple of sheets of newspaper down on the surface, then place the fish in the centre of the paper. For a round fish, cut the fish open along from the vent to the head. remove the entrails and rinse the cavity clean. Use a slightly salted fingertip to rub away any black membrane or blood clots from the cavity; the salt will allow you to get a good grip on the fish. For a flat fish, slit the fish behind the gills, squeeze out the entrails and rinse thoroughly.

When all the fish are gutted, roll up the entrails in the newspaper and discard. Do not use the entrails for making stock as blood will turn the stock cloudy.

Removing the Scales

To scale a fish, soak it in cold water for 2 minutes, then lay it on to a clean work surface. Hold the damp fish firmly with salted fingers by the tail and, using the back of a knife at 45 degrees, scrape off the scales from tail to head (the opposite way to the direction the scales lie). Once the scales are removed, turn the fish over and remove the scales from the other side. Rinse the fish under cold running water and pat dry on kitchen paper

Removing the Head and Tail
Remove the heads, fins and tails, if you wish, using a sharp knife or scissors.

If you are cooking a salmon ready to be dressed and served whole, leave the head and tail on and sprinkle them with salt as this helps to prevent burning when cooking.

If you are going to fillet the fish, remove the head but leave the tail.

If the fish is to be used whole, simply cut off the head carefully by scoring round the head then cutting through using a sharp knife or scissors. Remove the tail and fins using kitchen scissors.

Boning a Round Fish
This is the technique for round fish such as herrings, mackerel and trout, once you have gutted the fish and removed the head.

Make sure the split goes right to the tail. Place the fish skin-side up on to a board, pulling the cavity gently open. Press down firmly down the back bone in the middle of the fish along the length from the head to the tail so the cavity flattens on the board. Turn the fish over and gently peel off the backbone. Cut off the tail, using scissors or a knife. Using a pair of tweezers or pointed pliers, pull out and discard any remaining bones, feeling the surface lightly to locate them.

Filleting a Flat Fish
Place the fish on a board. Using a sharp knife, cut right down the centre of the fish to the bone, then make a small cut across the tail. Resting the tip of the knife on the bone, slide the knife down the length of the fish twice, then sweep the knife under the fillet until it lifts away. Repeat with the remaining fillets.

Skinning Fish

To skin a whole fish, rinse the fish, then cut away the fins using a pair of scissors. Make a small cut across the tail. Slip a finger underneath the skin and loosen the flesh and the dark skin around the sides of the fish. Salt your fingers with table salt, then hold the fish down firmly with one hand and hold the skin with the other hand. Pull the skin upward towards the head.

To skin a fillet of fish, lay it skin-side down on the work surface and salt your fingers. Using a sharp filleting knife, insert the blade between the skin and the flesh at the head end, then work towards the tail using a side-to-side sawing motion while pressing the flat side of the blade against the skin in order to keep the edge of the blade as close to the skin as possible.

Cooking Fish

One golden rule is never to overcook fish, Too much heat will squeeze out the natural juices and make the fish tough and flavourless. As soon as the fish turn opaque, it is cooked.

To test if the fish is cooked, simply insert a knife into the thickest part of the fish and it should just generally flake away in layers.

Grilling

This method is ideal for small fish, thin fillets and thicker cuts like plaice, sole, salmon, haddock, herring and mackerel.

Always preheat the grill before cooking, then cook under a moderate heat.

Brush white fish, like cod or pollock, with a little oil before cooking to prevent them drying out before they are cooked. It is not necessary to use oil on oily fish such as mackerel or herring. With round fish like herring, it helps to make two or three diagonal slashes on each side of the fish before you cook it.

Thin fillets only require cooking on one side; they will take about 5 minutes. Thick cutlets require cooking on one side, then turning over once during cooking to ensure that the fish is cooked through. You need to allow about 10–15 minutes for steaks or thick fillets.

Steaming

Steaming is ideal for fish like trout, plaice, sole, mussels or small whole fish.

Line a steamer with a piece of oiled or buttered foil to keep in the flavour. If you don't have a steamer, line a metal colander placed over a pan of water. Bring the water to simmering point.

Season the fish, then place in the steamer or colander and cover with a tight-fitting lid. Steam for about 5–10 minutes for thin pieces of fish to 15–20 minutes for thicker pieces of fish, just until the fish flakes.

If you like, you can add the steaming juices to a Béchamel Sauce (page 148) for added flavour.

You can also seal the fish in a baking parchment envelope to steam it.

Microwave Cooking

Any type of fish cooks really well in a microwave, although it does cook quickly so you need to be careful not to overcook.

Ideally cook the fish in a covered dish, or a baking parchment envelope, and use less liquid than you would for other cooking methods. Always season fish after cooking. Follow the manufacturer's timings for cooking fish or shellfish as microwave ovens vary considerably. As a guide, you'll need 5–10 minutes.

Shallow-frying

Fish cooks well by this method, which is ideal for all types of fish, including favourites like cod and bream as well as more unusual varieties such as pike or parrot fish.

Coat the prepared fish in a little seasoned flour. Heat a heavy-based frying pan with a little rapeseed oil or melted clarified butter. Add the fish and fry carefully for 4–5 minutes for small pieces of fish or about 10 minutes for large pieces. Turn the fish over once during cooking.

Deep-frying

This method is a moist way of cooking but high in calories. It is ideal for fillets of fish coated in batter or breadcrumbs. Do be very careful with this method of cooking as the oil gets very hot.

Make sure that the fish contains no water otherwise it with spit; ideally, pat the fish dry on kitchen paper. Coat the fish in seasoned flour, then in batter or egg and breadcrumbs.

Fill a deep-fat fryer just one-third full of vegetable oil and heat the oil to 190°C. To prevent fish sticking to the basket simply lower the basket slowly into the oil then take it out of the oil. Put the fish into the basket and cook for about 4–5 minutes or until the coating is crisp and golden brown. Drain on kitchen paper before serving.

Barbecuing
Barbecuing imparts a lovely smoky flavour to fish. It is ideal for large pieces of fish, such as mackerel or sea bass as well as shell fish like mussels.

To keep in the juices and avoid losing any of the fish through the mesh, you can lay the fish on a piece of baking parchment, then wrap it in foil before placing on the grill. You can also use a fish-shaped mesh holder, or create kebabs using firm seafood, brush with oil, then barbecue until just cooked. Cooking times will vary considerably depending on the size of the fish and the temperature of the coals.

Baking
Baking is best for larger pieces of fish, like whole salmon, herring, trout, plaice and sea bass.

For this method, it is also best to place the fish on a piece of baking parchment, then wrap it in foil and place it on to a deep sided baking tray. The fish will then cook in its own juices and maintain all its wonderful flavour. Bake in the oven at 180°C/gas 4 for 15–30 minutes for smaller pieces of fish or about 40–50 minutes for a large fish.

It's all in the can

Canned fish is a great standby in the store cupboard. The ingredients are sealed in the can and the fish is commercially cooked in the can so that bacteria are sealed out but the seafood's vitamins and minerals are sealed in.

You can now find a wonderful array of canned products, like anchovy fillets, mussels, salmon, oysters and sardines in a variety of different sauces, so there are plenty of options available.

Canned fish keeps longer than other preserved foods, you should keep an eye on the use-by date and rotate your stock, especially checking that they show no signs of rust, denting or 'blowing' at the seam, which means the contents could be damaged.

Once opened canned food should be treated as for fresh. The contents should be poured into a covered non-metallic container and used within a couple of days. Never keep opened cans in the fridge; the contents of the can will start to oxidise and eat into the lining of the can, giving the food a metallic taste.

Canned fish make an nutritious snack as a filling for a sandwich or omelette, to stir through pasta or toss into your favourite salad.

Troubleshooting

Although fish is easy to cook, if you do encounter problems, you may find the solutions here.

White fish has gone dry during cooking: This may happen if the fish is overcooked or cooked by an incorrect method, such as grilling for fish that is too delicate, which can have a drying effect. Allowing the fish to marinate will help to keep the fish moist.

Shellfish has gone very dry and rubbery: This could be either that the fish was overcooked, as shellfish cooks very quickly, especially if the sizes of the fish were inconsistent so some have cooked before others.

The coating has not stuck on the fish during cooking: Make sure the fish is dry before coating in batter or breadcrumbs.

The fish has fallen apart during cooking: The fish may have been over-handled or overcooked. Also make sure you turn it carefully using a fish slice.

CHAPTER 1

Soups and Starters

Here is a collection of delicious soups and starters which you can serve to introduce your meal, or as snacks or light meals in their own right.

Soups are always popular, and fish soups can be particularly delicate and subtly flavoured. Make sure hot soups are served piping hot, and cold soups are served well chilled.

Especially if you are serving a large number of people, try to choose a starter that you can make in advance and place on the table before your guests sit down. That way, you get to spend more time with them and will have time to add the finishing touches to the main course.

Starters are generally light and served in small portions. They should not be overwhelming, because they are designed to stimulate the appetite and set the scene for the rest of the meal. As such, they should always be attractively presented and served. One golden rule is to make sure that the starter does not include the same ingredients as the courses that follow.

Huss and Rocket Soup

600ml milk
1 tsp mixed dried herbs
2 shallots, finely chopped
250g huss, cut into chunks
125g rocket
150ml single cream

To garnish
A few small rocket leaves
Croûtons (page 156)

You might think this a surprising combination but it makes a delicious soup. Huss has several names, including rockfish and dogfish. It is quite a sweet fish with a soft bone down the centre and no sharp bones.

- Put the milk, dried herbs and shallots in a pan. Add the huss and rocket and bring to the boil.

- Reduce the heat and simmer for 8–10 minutes or until the fish flakes when tested with a fork.

- Remove and discard any bones.

- Place the fish in a food processor with the cream and process until smooth.

- Return to the pan and heat gently but do not allow to boil.

- Serve the soup in individual soup bowls garnished with rocket leaves and croûtons.

Smoked Haddock Chowder

SERVES 4

A chowder is a thick soup made with onion, milk and potato. In this case, I've used delicious smoked haddock. You can serve this heart-warming soup with chunks of crusty bread to make a complete meal.

- Wipe the fish with kitchen paper and cut into 4cm pieces. Remove and discard any bones.

- In a heavy-based pan, heat the butter and fry the onion for 2–3 minutes until just soft, then add the celery, potato, carrot, garlic and water. Season to taste. Bring to the boil, then simmer for about 10 minutes.

- Pour in the milk and heat gently. Taste and season well.

- Ladle the soup into hot soup bowls and garnish with sprigs of fresh parsley. Serve with crusty bread of your choice.

350g natural smoked haddock, skinned
25g unsalted butter
1 onion, finely chopped
1 celery stick, finely chopped
300g potato, peeled and diced into 2.5cm pieces
1 small carrot, finely chopped
1 garlic clove, chopped
300ml boiling water
Salt and freshly ground black pepper
300ml whole milk

To garnish
Sprigs of fresh flatleaf parsley

To serve
Crusty bread

New England Chowder

50g butter
4 spring onions, chopped
40g plain flour
Pinch of cayenne pepper
Freshly ground black
  pepper
600ml Fish Stock
  (page 142)
180g can of clams
125g peeled prawns,
  thawed if frozen
198g can of sweetcorn
2 potatoes, peeled and
  diced
150ml soured cream

To garnish
1 tbsp chopped fresh
  parsley

Ideal for a cold winter's day, this is a very filling soup that is easily made from ingredients you are likely to have in the cupboard. I like to serve it with chunks of warm crusty bread.

- Melt the butter in a heavy-based pan, stir in the spring onions and cook for 2–3 minutes.

- Stir in the flour and cayenne pepper, then season to taste with black pepper and cook for 2 minutes.

- Slowly add the stock, then bring the soup to the boil.

- Add the clams, prawns, sweetcorn and potatoes and simmer for 15 minutes or until the potatoes are cooked.

- Stir in the soured cream and garnish with a sprinkling of parsley to serve.

Anything Goes Fresh Fish Soup

SERVES 4

As the name suggests, you can use any kind of fish or seafood to make this soup so try your own variations and see what you like best. It does not take long to make but the taste is just amazing.

- Heat the oil in a large pan, add the leek, garlic, celery, fennel and chilli and fry for 5–8 minutes or until the vegetables have just started to soften, stirring all the time.

- Pour in the stock and white wine, bring to the boil and skim the surface if necessary. Reduce the heat and simmer for 5 minutes.

- Add the large pieces of fish first, then add the tomatoes and thyme. Simmer for 5–10 minutes until the white fish is just cooked.

- Add the remaining fish and cook for a further 2 minutes or until the mussels are opened. Discard any mussels that have remained closed.

- Season to taste, then ladle into soup bowls and serve with crusty French bread.

2–3 tbsp rapeseed oil
1 small leek, thinly sliced
2 large garlic cloves, finely crushed
3 celery sticks, thinly sliced
1 small fennel bulb, thinly sliced
1 small red chilli, deseeded and finely chopped (optional)
1 litre Fish Stock (page 142)
4 tbsp white wine
700g mixed fish like unpeeled prawns, mussels, pollock, cod or coley, cut into large pieces
3 large beef tomatoes, chopped
4 sprigs of fresh thyme
Salt and freshly ground black pepper

To serve
Crusty French bread

Smoked Mackerel with Fennel Seeds

1 tsp fennel seeds
200g smoked mackerel,
  skinned, boned and
  broken into pieces
180g cream cheese
1–2 tsp fresh lemon juice
4 tbsp crème fraîche
2 tbsp creamy horseradish
  sauce
2 tsp snipped fresh chives
Freshly ground black
  pepper

To serve
Bread sticks or triangles
  of brown bread

A delightful recipe, this can be served as an elegant starter or simply offered to guests as a nibble with drinks. It tastes at its best when well chilled, so make it in advance to allow enough time for it to chill.

- Dry-fry the fennel seeds in a non-stick pan for 1–2 minutes or until they start to turn golden and they smell of aniseed. Remove from the heat immediately and leave to cool.

- When cold, grind them coarsely in a pestle and mortar.

- In a food processor or in a bowl using a hand blender, blend the mackerel, cream cheese, lemon juice, crème fraîche, ground fennel seeds, horseradish and chives until smooth or to the required consistency.

- Transfer to a serving dish, cover with clingfilm and chill for 1–2 hours before serving with bread sticks or triangles of brown bread.

Gravadlax

This is a Swedish dish of salmon prepared in salt and sugar that is absolutely delicious, although very simple to make. It is served usually as a starter with lemon wedges and thin slices of brown bread.

- Make sure that all the small bones are taken out of the salmon. Clean the fillet and pat dry with kitchen paper. Put one fillet skin-side down in a glass or ceramic dish.

- In a bowl, mix together the dill, salt, sugar and peppercorns.

- Spread the mixture over the fillet in the dish and then place the other one on top. Cover the fish with clingfilm and weigh it down with clean cans or weights.

- Chill in the fridge for 2 days basting the fish every 10 hours.

- Remove the salmon from the brine mixture and use a filleting knife to slice it thinly, making sure the skin remains intact.

- Garnish with the dill sprigs and serve with lemon wedges and slices of brown bread.

SERVES 10-12

2 x 500g salmon fillets, with the skin on but descaled
6 tbsp chopped fresh dill, plus a few sprigs to garnish
100g sea salt, coarsely ground
50g caster sugar
1 tbsp freshly ground white peppercorns

To serve
1 lemon, cut into wedges
Slices of brown bread

Sweet and Sour Prawns

75g soft brown sugar
60ml cider vinegar
45ml soy sauce
60ml tomato ketchup
2 tbsp cornflour
150ml pineapple juice
150ml water
227g can of bamboo
    shoots, drained
1 large green chilli,
    deseeded and thinly
    sliced (optional)
450g peeled prawns,
    thawed if frozen
Salt and freshly ground
    black pepper

To garnish
Whole, cooked, unpeeled
    prawns
1 lime, sliced
A few sprigs of fresh dill

A classic Chinese-style dish, this is a real favourite with so many people. It makes a delicious starter for six, or you can serve it as a main course for four, in which case you could serve it with a rice dish.

- Place the sugar, vinegar, soy sauce and tomato ketchup in a small pan.

- In a clean bowl, mix the cornflour with a little of the pineapple juice to make a loose paste, then stir in the remaining water and pineapple juice. Add it to the pan.

- Bring the ingredients to the boil, stirring constantly, then simmer gently for 5 minutes, whisking if necessary, until smooth.

- Add the bamboo shoots and simmer for a further 2 minutes.

- Add the prawns and simmer for 8 minutes or until cooked through. Season to taste.

- Spoon the mixture on to a warmed serving dish and garnish with the whole prawns, slices of lime and sprigs of dill. Serve immediately.

Sesame Prawn Toasts

SERVES 4

This popular little starter or snack is made from toast topped with a tasty prawn paste and a coating of sesame seeds. I think the flavour of home-made prawn toasts is better than ready-mades. Serve them with a sweet chilli dipping sauce.

350g cooked, peeled prawns
1 egg
3–4 spring onions, finely chopped
2 tsp finely chopped fresh root ginger
1 tbsp light soy sauce
1 tsp sesame oil
Pinch of salt
8 thin slices of white bread, crusts removed
4–6 tbsp sesame seeds
Vegetable oil, for frying

- Place the prawns, egg, spring onions, ginger, soy sauce, sesame oil and salt in a blender or food processor and process to a paste.

- Spread the prawn purée thickly and evenly over the bread.

- Sprinkle the sesame seeds on a plate, then turn the bread slices over and gently press the seeds on to the purée to coat evenly.

- Heat a heavy-based frying pan or wok filled with 2.5cm oil and fry the toasts sesame-sides down for about 1 minute or until crisp and golden brown.

- Turn them over and fry the other side until golden brown, then drain on kitchen paper.

- Cut each slice into even strips or triangles and serve immediately.

To vary
Replace the prawns with crab sticks or off-cuts of farmed salmon.

Smoked Trout Pâté

175g smoked trout
75g unsalted butter,
   at room temperature
1–2 tbsp fresh lemon juice
50ml single cream or
   Greek yoghurt
A little freshly ground
   black pepper

To garnish
A few sprigs of fresh dill

This dish is so easy and inexpensive to make, especially if you use smoked trout trimmings. Smoked salmon or mackerel can be used in place of the trout, but do make sure all the bones and skin are discarded.

- Cut the trout into small dice, reserving 4–6 pieces for garnishing. Blend the trout in a food processor with the butter, lemon juice and cream until smooth. Season to taste.

- Spoon the mixture into 4–6 small ramekins and chill well.

- Serve garnished with the remaining trout strips and sprigs of dill.

To vary
If you are using smoked mackerel, flavour the pâté with 1–2 tbsp creamed horseradish sauce.

Potted Shrimps

This takes about half an hour to make but is worth every minute. Shrimps from the Irish Sea and English Channel are mainly brown and have a better flavour than the pink variety, although they are expensive if you buy them peeled and prepared.

- Mix the shrimps with the lemon juice, nutmeg and pepper to taste.

- Spoon the shrimps into 4 ramekins and smooth the surface.

- Pour the melted butter evenly over the shrimps.

- Garnish with lime or lemon slices and serve with buttered brown bread or toast.

To vary
Replace the shrimps with prawns, smoked trout, white crab meat or salmon.

225g peeled shrimps
1–2 tsp fresh lemon juice, to taste
Pinch of freshly grated nutmeg or ground mace (optional)
Freshly ground black pepper
75g unsalted butter, melted

To garnish
A few slices of lemon or lime

To serve
Freshly buttered brown bread or toast

Oysters

16 oysters
Crushed ice
Salt and freshly ground
   black pepper

To serve
Brown bread and butter
1 lemon, cut into wedges
Tabasco sauce

Oysters used to be cheap and plentiful but have become quite exclusive, which is a shame because they are easy to prepare and have become more reasonably priced. Store them out of water in the base of the fridge and use on the day of purchase.

- Scrub the oysters well and discard any beards and seaweed. The oysters should be firmly closed; discard any that are open and do not close when tapped.

- To serve the oysters raw, hold each one in a thick cloth or glove in the palm of one hand and prise open the shells at the hinge using an oyster knife. Loosen the oyster from the shell, leaving it in one deeper half shell. Season lightly.

- Serve with brown bread, lemon wedges and Tabasco sauce.

The Best Prawn Cocktail

There's a reason why this starter has remained so popular. Don't dismiss it as a retro throwback! Try this version made with home-made mayonnaise, served well chilled and garnished with lemons wedges and whole unpeeled prawns.

- Place the lettuce in the base of 4 serving dishes.

- In a bowl, mix together the mayonnaise, cream or yoghurt, ketchup, lemon juice and Tabasco sauce. Season to taste.

- Divide the prawns evenly between the dishes, arranging on top of the lettuce, then spoon over the sauce.

- Cover and chill for 30–45 minutes before serving.

- Just before serving, sprinkle with a little paprika and garnish with the prawns and lemon wedges.

¼ iceberg lettuce, finely shredded
150ml mayonnaise (page 143)
2 tbsp whipping cream or thick Greek yoghurt
2–3 tbsp tomato ketchup
2 tbsp fresh lemon juice
A few drops of Tabasco sauce
Salt and freshly ground black pepper
300g peeled cooked prawns, thawed if frozen

To garnish
4 lemon wedges
8 whole prawns
A little ground paprika

Cook's tip
To get the best results, try to use fresh unpeeled prawns from the fish counter as these give a better flavour. Frozen prawns seems to lose their flavour when they thaw out. Do make sure the prawns are cooked ones.

Thai Fish Cakes

2 dried chillies, halved lengthways and seeded
1 banana shallot, finely chopped
1 garlic clove, chopped
25g coriander sprigs, chopped
6 dried kaffir lime leaves
Salt
450g coley, skinned and boned
2 tbsp Thai fish sauce
50g French beans, finely chopped
Rapeseed oil, for deep-frying
125ml rice wine vinegar
2–3 tbsp sugar
¼ cucumber, halved and sliced
1 carrot, very finely chopped
3 banana shallots, very thinly sliced
1 chilli, seeded and finely chopped
100g freshly roasted shelled ground nuts

This uses off-cuts of fish like cod, coley or pollock. Instead of making your own Thai paste, buy a jar of good-quality paste. You can also use Thai red curry paste instead of the kaffir lime leaves and salt. To serve as a main course, double the quantity.

- Make the spice mixture by blending together the chillies, shallot, garlic, coriander, lime leaves and salt in a mini processor or in a pestle and mortar.

- Process the fish in food processor, then transfer to a bowl.

- Add 1 tbsp of the paste to the fish and use your fingers to blend thoroughly. Add the fish sauce and beans and mix well.

- Make into 7cm, flat cakes about 1cm thick and chill until ready to serve.

- To make the sauce, gently heat the wine vinegar and sugar, to taste, until the sugar has dissolved, then bring to the boil and boil for 1 minute to form a syrup. Leave to cool.

- When the syrup is cold, add the cucumber, carrot, shallots and chilli and mix well together. Sprinkle on the nuts.

- Heat the oil in a deep-fat fryer or pan to 190°C, one third full.

- Fry the fish cakes a few at a time for about 5 minutes or until golden, then drain on kitchen paper.

- Arrange the fish cakes on top of the salad to serve.

Prawns in Ginger and Garlic Sauce

2 tbsp vegetable oil
450g raw tiger prawns in their shells
2 tsp finely chopped fresh ginger
1 large garlic clove, crushed
2 spring onions, thinly sliced
1–2 tbsp chilli bean sauce
2 tsp chicken stock
1 tsp rice wine vinegar
1 tsp light soy sauce
Pinch of sugar

This is a great way to serve whole tiger prawns: with a hint of ginger and oriental spices cooked quickly in a wok. Serve with a finger bowl as this is a delightfully messy dish to eat with your fingers.

● Preheat a wok or a large, heavy-based frying pan.

● Add the prawns and stir-fry for 4–5 minutes until just cooked – they will turn pink – then remove them from the pan and keep them hot.

● Add the ginger and garlic to the pan and cook for 1 minute.

● Add the spring onions and chilli bean sauce. Return the prawns to the pan and stir to coat in the sauce. Add the stock, wine vinegar, soy sauce and sugar.

● Lift out the prawns with a slotted spoon and place on serving plates. Pour the sauce into a small bowl to serve with the prawns.

Whiting Provençal

Whiting, along with many other small fish, can be caught with a net or small line from piers and boats. Whiting are easy to recognise as they have a silver skin with a thin brown line running down the side. This makes a delicious starter or light lunch.

- Slash the fish diagonally 3 times on each side.

- Fry the onions in the oil for 2–3 minutes until just soft in a heavy-based frying pan. Add the tomatoes and herbs stir well.

- Put the fish on top of the tomato mixture. Cook for 10–15 minutes or until cooked on both sides.

4 small whiting, skinned and heads removed
2 large onions, chopped
4 tbsp oil
4 tomatoes, chopped
2 tbsp chopped fresh parsley

Scallop and Mushroom Tartlets

For the pastry
225g plain flour
Pinch of salt
100g butter or hard
   cooking margarine
1 egg yolk
A little cold water

For the filling
50g butter
175g button mushrooms,
   sliced
12 small or 8 large scallops
1 tbsp fresh lemon juice
1 tbsp chopped fresh dill
Salt and freshly ground
   black pepper

To garnish
1 lemon, cut into wedges
Sprigs of dill

These tartlets can be made from larger (king) scallops or the delicate small ones known as queenies; these are now sustainably farmed. The beautifully tender scallops contrast perfectly with the crisp pastry cases, making these an ideal starter.

- Sift the flour and salt into a mixing bowl and rub in the butter or margarine until the mixture forms fine breadcrumbs.

- Add the egg yolk and enough cold water to make a firm, rolling consistency, then wrap in clingfilm and put in the fridge for 30 minutes.

- Heat the oven to 200°C/gas 6 and grease 12 fairly large patty tins or individual tartlet tins.

- Roll out the dough on a lightly floured surface and cut out into rounds to fit the tins. Line the tins with the pastry and prick all over with a fork, then bake in the oven for 12–15 minutes until crisp and golden.

- Meanwhile, make the filling. Heat the butter in a frying pan, add the mushrooms and cook for 5 minutes.

- Cut large scallops into small pieces but leave queenies whole. Add the scallops to the pan with the lemon juice and dill. Season to taste. Cook for 3–4 minutes only, stirring frequently.

- Spoon the hot filling into the cases and serve garnished with lemon wedges and sprigs of dill.

To vary
These tartlets are equally good served cold. Cook the scallops and the mushrooms as above. Allow to cool, then blend the filling with a little thick natural yoghurt or whipping cream before dividing between the cold tartlets.

CHAPTER 2

Brunches and Snacks

We are always told that breakfast is the most important meal of the day. For most of us, an ordinary weekdays breakfast is usually a fairly rushed bowl of cereal or perhaps a slice of toast with fruit juice or a coffee. So when you have time to be a bit more leisurely and make a cooked breakfast or brunch, remember how light and nutritious fish can be – which perfectly fits the bill – and that it is also quick to prepare and cook.

Many of these recipes are traditional breakfast or brunch dishes but many make equally good snacks or starters.

Smoked Salmon Sunday Brunch Bagel

What a great way to relax on a Sunday morning, with the papers spread out in front of you, no deadlines to meet, a glass of freshly squeezed orange juice and a mug of freshly made coffee.

- Toast the bagels until golden brown.

- Meanwhile, heat a frying pan, add the salmon slices and cook gently for 1–2 minutes until opaque.

- Blend the mayonnaise with the horseradish and season to taste.

- Top the bagel with the salmon and poached eggs. Season with freshly grated black pepper.

- Garnish with the dill and anchovy fillets and serve with the mayonnaise on the side.

4 bagels, cut in half
  horizontally
4 slices of smoked salmon
  or trout
4 tbsp mayonnaise
  (page 143)
2 tsp creamy horseradish
Salt and freshly ground
  black pepper
4 freshly cooked poached
  eggs
1–2 anchovies fillets,
  halved lengthways

To garnish
Fresh dill sprigs

Herring and Dill Bagel

2 bagels, cut in half
   horizontally
A little butter
200g skinned and pickled
   herrings with onion
3 tbsp thick Greek 10%
   fat yoghurt
1 tbsp chopped fresh dill
Freshly ground black
   pepper

To garnish
Lemon wedges
Fresh dill sprigs

This is a treat for all lovers of herring: a freshly toasted bagel with a creamy topping. Buy the herrings from the deli counter at the supermarket or in the fish section with the canned fish.

- Cut the bagel in half horizontally and toast on both sides. Lightly butter the toasted surfaces.

- In a bowl, mix together the herring fillets, yoghurt, dill and pepper. Spoon the herring mixture on to the bagel halves and serve garnished with lemon wedges and dill.

Grilled Kippers

This is a traditional Victorian breakfast dish that has gone out of fashion now breakfasts are not such a splendid affair! They make a great brunch, though, and are simple and quick to make.

- Line the grill pan with foil and brush the foil with melted butter. Preheat the grill to medium hot.

- Place the fish on the foil, skin-side up and grill for 1 minute, turn them over, brush the flesh with melted butter and grill for a further 4–5 minutes until the butter is bubbling.

- Sprinkle with a dash of cayenne and serve immediately with lemon wedges so you can squeeze the juice over the top.

25g butter, melted
4 kipper fillets

To serve
Cayenne pepper
1 lemon, cut into wedges

Marinated Kippers

8 kipper fillets
1 onion, very thinly sliced
6 black peppercorns
2 bay leaves
6 tbsp rapeseed oil
3 tbsp cider vinegar

To serve
Brown bread and butter

The best kippers you can find in the UK come from the Isle of Man; they are plump and very fleshy with a wonderful flavour. Seek them out if you can – although I'm sure you'll enjoy this dish with any kippers as it is ideal for a lazy brunch.

- With a filleting knife, remove the skin off the kippers and carefully take out and discard any small bones with a pair of tweezers.

- Place the kippers in a non-metallic dish with the onion, peppercorns and bay leaves. Spoon over the oil and vinegar, cover and leave to marinate for 24 hours, turning once.

- Serve chilled with brown bread.

Smoky Kedgeree

SERVES 6

This is a delightful brunch dish made with smoked fish. What can be nicer than sitting down with the Sunday newspaper and tucking into a lovely dish of rice with that aromatic smoky flavour and a host of delicious ingredients.

- Peel, halve and stone the avocado, then slice it and dip in lemon juice.

- Heat the oil in a large frying pan. Add the rice and spring onions and stir-fry for 1 minute or until the grain are coated and shiny.

- Stir in the ground turmeric, chicken or fish stock and peas and season to taste.

- Reduce the heat, cover and simmer for 10 minutes or until the rice is just tender.

- Slice the egg into wedges.

- Add the butter and cream to the rice and stir well. Add the flaked trout, eggs and avocado slices.

- Garnish with small pieces of dill to serve.

1 small, ripe avocado
2 tbsp lemon juice
2 tbsp rapeseed oil
175g long-grain rice, rinsed well
1 bunch of spring onions, cut into 2.5cm pieces
½ tsp ground turmeric
450ml Fish Stock (page 142) or chicken stock
50g frozen peas
Salt and freshly ground black pepper
2 eggs, hard-boiled and shelled
25g unsalted butter
150ml single cream
450g smoked trout fillet, skinned and flaked

To garnish
Sprigs of fresh dill

To vary
You could replace the smoked trout with boned and flaked smoked mackerel. Stir some chopped fresh parsley into the dish instead of the dill.

Smoked Salmon Scramble

4 slices of freshly baked
   brown bread
100g unsalted butter
12 eggs
A little black pepper
2 tbsp double cream
100g thinly sliced smoked
   salmon, cut into short
   strips

To garnish
Small parsley sprigs
1 lemon, cut into wedges

This is one of my favourite weekend dishes, especially if I feel like spoiling myself. To cut down the cost, use smoked salmon off-cuts, which are available at most supermarkets. Ideally use the freshest eggs you can.

● Toast the bread, then cut off the crusts and spread the slices with butter. Cut each piece of toast into 6 triangles by cutting off each corner of the square midway between one corner and the next. Cut the square of toast that remains in half.

● Break the eggs into a bowl and whisk together with the seasoning.

● Melt the remaining butter in the pan and add the eggs. Stir with a wooden spoon, scraping the cooked egg away from the base of the pan until the degree of firmness you like is achieved.

● Remove the pan from the heat and stir in the cream, then fold in the smoked salmon.

● Garnish with parsley sprigs and serve with lemon wedges and the hot buttered toast.

To vary
Spread the toast with soft cream cheese with herbs instead of the butter.

Prawn and Mangetout Omelette

SERVES 4

This is a speedy brunch omelette that is simple to make and delicious to eat. The dash of sweet chilli sauce lifts the flavours and complements the oriental style. It is also good with Melba toast.

4 tsp rapeseed oil
300g raw, peeled king prawn tails
1 bunch of spring onions, thinly sliced
75–100g mangetout, halved
8 eggs, beaten
4 tbsp sweet chilli sauce

To serve
Hot buttered toast
Crispy salad

- Heat 1 tsp of the oil in a 20cm non-stick pan.

- Add the prawns and stir-fry for 1–2 minutes. Add the remaining oil.

- Add the onions and mangetout and cook for a few minutes or until the prawns turn pink.

- Take out and reserve three-quarters of the prawn mixture.

- Add one quarter of the beaten egg to the pan, stir into the remaining prawn mixture and cook for 2 minutes until the base is set and golden. Turn them over and cook the other side. Drizzle over the chilli sauce.

- Transfer the first omelette to a warm place while you make 3 more omelettes in the same way.

- Serve with hot buttered toast and a crisp salad garnish.

Soft Herring Roes on Toast

8 soft herring roes,
cleaned and dried
Salt and freshly ground
black pepper
A little plain flour
75g butter, at room
temperature
15g capers, well drained
and finely chopped
(optional)
1 small shallot, very
finely chopped

To serve
4 slices of toast
1 lemon, cut into wedges

Allow two herring roes per person or use one well-drained 200g can; if you use frozen, make sure they are completely defrosted. I used to enjoy this little tea-time delicacy with hot buttered toast midweek or for a weekend breakfast.

- Season the roes and dust with a little flour.

- Melt 50g of the butter in a frying pan, then add the roes and fry gently for a few minutes until golden brown. Remove from the pan and keep warm.

- In a bowl, mix the remaining butter with the capers and shallot, then season to taste.

- Add to the pan and fry for a few minutes until the shallot is just soft.

- Arrange the roes on the slices of toast and drizzle the sauce over the top. Serve garnished with lemon wedges.

Garlic Prawns

One of the best ways to serve prawns is in a rich, buttery sauce flavoured simply with garlic and lemon juice. It takes only minutes to prepare so makes the perfect snack, or can be served as a starter for everyday or to enjoy with friends.

- In a large, heavy-based pan, slowly melt the butter.

- Add the garlic and fry for about half a minute.

- Add the prawns and pepper and cook for about 2–3 minutes, then turn them over and cook for a further 3 minutes.

- Stir in the parsley, lemon juice and a little more pepper to taste.

- Serve with the salad and crusty French bread.

100g unsalted butter
3 garlic cloves, crushed
24 raw tiger prawns, cleaned, deveined and thawed if frozen
Freshly ground black pepper
1 tbsp chopped fresh flatleaf parsley,
2 tbsp lemon juice

To serve
Mixed baby leaf salad
Crusty French bread

Oysters with Sun-dried Tomato Cream

12 oysters, shucked
(make sure all the
shell is removed)
2 banana shallots, finely
chopped
275ml double or
whipping cream
4 sun-dried tomatoes,
drained and chopped
1 tbsp finely snipped
chives
25g dried white
breadcrumbs (ready
prepared or
home-made)
30g Parmesan cheese,
grated
A few drops of Tabasco
sauce or a large pinch
of cayenne pepper

To garnish
A few fresh chives

The price of farmed oysters has gone down considerably over the past few years. To 'shuck' oysters means to loosen them from their shells. Ideally you need thick gloves and an oysters knife, so instead, ask your fishmonger to shuck the oysters for you.

- Drain the oysters, reserving the natural juice. Strain into a little bowl. Discard the flat shells and keep the concave ones. Clean the shells and discard any loose shell. Put the oysters back into the shells and arrange on a flameproof plate.

- Place the shallots and cream in a small pan and bring to the boil, then simmer for about 8 minutes until reduced by half. Leave to cool.

- Stir in the sun-dried tomatoes and chives. Spoon the sauce over the oysters.

- In a bowl, mix the breadcrumbs with the Parmesan and Tabasco or cayenne pepper, then sprinkle it over the oysters.

- Put under a preheated grill for 30–60 seconds until bubbling and golden brown. Garnish with lengths of chives and serve at once.

To vary
Use a 10% fat natural Greek yoghurt to replace the cream.

South Coast Scallops with Basil Pesto

A really delightful way to serve king scallops, but do try to buy those that have been collected by hand, or sustainably farmed, as they do not damage the precious habitats. They are a little more expensive but we are helping to save the seas around us.

For the pesto
150g basil, leaves, wild garlic or wild rocket leaves
1 small garlic clove, crushed
6 tbsp olive oil
1 tbsp balsamic vinegar

For the scallops
50g fresh basil
10 baby plum tomatoes, quartered
6 tbsp olive oil
12 fresh scallops with roe, out of their shells
Salt and freshly ground black pepper
4 slices of ciabatta bread, sliced diagonally and toasted
2 garlic cloves, crushed

- In a food processor or blender, process all the pesto ingredients until well blended.

- Tear the basil finely into a bowl, or chop it finely. Add the tomatoes and 4 tbsp of the oil.

- Dip the scallops in the remaining oil on both sides and season them well.

- Preheat a frying or ridged griddle pan and cook the scallops for 1½ minutes each side.

- Rub the toast with the crushed garlic.

- Divide the pesto evenly between serving plates. Put 3 scallops on to each slice of the bread and serve immediately with the tomato mixture.

Smoked Pin Wheels

SERVES 6–8

These bite-sized treats make a lovely snack to serve to guests with a glass of chilled white wine, or you can serve them as a starter. They can be made in advance and wrapped in clingfilm.

½ brown loaf, sliced and crusts removed
50g unsalted butter, at room temperature
175g smoked trout, thinly sliced
1 lemon, halved
A little ground black pepper

- Butter each slice of bread and cover with smoked trout. Sprinkle with a little lemon juice and season with pepper.

- Roll up the bread to form a wheel then wrap in clingfilm and chill in the fridge for 1–2 hours.

- Cut through into even-sized slices.

To vary
Replace the butter with either softened goats' cheese or soft cream cheese. Garnish with small sprigs of dill or snipped chives. If you like, you can use smoked salmon in place of smoked trout.

Coley Goujons

3–4 tbsp plain flour
Salt and freshly ground
   black pepper
450g coley, skinned and
   cut into 20 even-sized
   pieces
Oil, for deep-frying
1 egg, beaten
50g fresh white
   breadcrumbs

To serve
Tomato sauce

A great economical family treat made from coley, you can use this fish to replace your favourite cod recipe. The pinkish-grey meaty flesh turns white when cooked and is juicy and tender.

- Season the flour and place it in a polythene bag. Add the fish and toss the fish in the flour to coat.

- Remove the fish from the bag and shake off any excess flour.

- Heat the oil to 180°C.

- Dip the fish into the egg, then the breadcrumbs, making sure that all the excess crumbs are shaken off.

- Carefully lower the fish into the hot oil and fry for a few minutes until golden brown. Drain on kitchen paper.

- Serve the goujons on cocktail sticks with tomato sauce to dip into.

To vary
Replace the coley with haddock, boned and filleted, sand dabs or plaice cut into even strips.

Trout Dippers with Guacamole

SERVES 4

Use any fish you like for this quick and easy recipe because it works well with all kinds. Why not try pollock, sand dabs, hake or coley. The flavours of the fish work beautifully with the avocado.

- Put the hazelnuts, cornflour and parsley into a food processor, season, then process until the nuts are finely chopped.

- Dip the trout into the beaten egg, shake off the excess, then coat with the nut mixture.

- Fill a deep-fat fryer or heavy-based pan one-third full of oil and heat to 180°C.

- Lower in the trout strips in the basket and fry for about 2–3 minutes or until cooked and the coating is golden brown.

- Drain the fish on crumpled kitchen paper.

- Toss the avocado in the lemon juice to prevent discoloration, then place in a food processor with the onion, crème fraîche and Worcestershire sauce. Season to taste and process until smooth.

- Spoon the mixture into a serving bowl and sprinkle over the paprika and chives.

- Arrange the trout strips on a serving plate and serve immediately with the guacamole.

100g shelled hazelnuts
2 tbsp cornflour
1 tbsp chopped fresh parsley
Salt and freshly ground black pepper
450g skinless trout fillets, cut into strips
1 egg, beaten
Vegetable oil, for frying
1 avocado, peeled, stoned and roughly chopped
30ml freshly squeezed lemon juice
½ small onion, roughly chopped
150ml crème fraîche
2 tsp Worcestershire sauce

To garnish
Ground paprika
Snipped fresh chives

Cheese and Tuna Melts

2 x 200g cans of tuna,
     drained
1 bunch of spring onions,
     sliced into 1cm pieces
4 tbsp mayonnaise
     (page 143)
6 slices of Granary, brown
     or white bread
100g strong Cheddar
     cheese, grated
A little ground paprika

To serve
Mixed salad

This tasty lunch or evening snack is made from canned tuna, which is a great standby to keep in the cupboard. It is quick and easy to make but creates a delicious and filling snack or a light lunch on its own or teamed with some salad.

- Preheat the grill to high.

- Flake the tuna into a bowl and mix in the spring onions and mayonnaise.

- Toast the bread until pale golden brown on both sides, then spread with the tuna mixture and scatter the cheese on top.

- Grill for 4–5 minutes until bubbling and golden brown.

- Sprinkle with paprika. Cut the melts in half and serve with a little seasonal salad.

To vary
Use up any leftover cooked fresh tuna for this recipe.

CHAPTER 3

Cold Lunches and Suppers

This selection of recipes includes some delicious salads and other dishes to be served cold as light summer suppers or tasty lunches. Some are also suitable for serving as starters, in which case you would usually use this quantity to serve six or eight, rather than four.

Remember to store seafood carefully, and do not leave a seafood salad waiting around out of the fridge for any length of time.

You can always experiment and vary the recipes using different types of fish.

Rocket, Avocado and Prawn Salad

1 small fresh red chilli,
  seeded and finely
  chopped
1 garlic clove, crushed
Grated zest and juice of
  ½ lemon
1 tbsp soy sauce
½ tbsp sesame oil
275g cooked, peeled
  prawns
140g bag of rocket,
  washed and drained
2 rich, firm avocados

To serve
French bread

A wonderful, quick salad with a hint of fresh chilli, this is ideal for a hot summer's day. If you prefer, you can replace the rocket with baby leaf spinach or pea shoots, or try it with your favourite salad leaves.

- Mix together the chilli, garlic, lemon juice and zest, soy sauce and sesame oil, then add the prawns, cover with clingfilm and chill for 1–2 hours.

- Lift out the prawns using a slotted spoon and put to one side.

- Toss the rocket in the remaining dressing, then add the prawns.

- Carefully cut the avocados in half and remove the stones. Peel and discard the skin and slice the flesh.

- Toss all the ingredients together carefully in the dressing, then and divide into 4 serving dishes. Serve with chunks fresh French bread.

Salade Niçoise

A Mediterranean-style dish, this is a salad of tuna, olives, beans and hard-boiled eggs that hails from the city of Nice on France's Côte d'Azur. These are the classic ingredients but you can adapt it to suit yourself. It will serve six as a starter.

- Flake the fish into bite-sized pieces.

- Arrange the fish, tomatoes, olives, cucumber, French beans and egg in a serving bowl.

- Sprinkle over the herbs and then pour over the dressing. Top with the anchovies, cover and leave to chill in the fridge for 30 minutes.

200g can of tuna, drained
225g tomatoes, cut into eighths
50g black olives, stoned and halved
½ small cucumber, sliced
200g French beans, blanched and drained well
3 hard-boiled eggs, shelled and quartered
1 tbsp chopped fresh parsley
8 anchovies, drained and halved lengthways

To serve
French Dressing (page 146)

To vary
Instead of using canned tuna, use fresh tuna instead. Use 4 tuna steaks, about 150g each. Baste the tuna in a very little olive oil and leave for 30 minutes. Heat a ridged frying pan until hot, then cook the steaks for 2 minutes on each side. Thick meaty fish is best served 'pink'. Remove the steaks from the heat and allow to stand for 5 minutes before proceeding as above.

Rollmop Herrings

4 herring fillets
Salt and freshly ground
    black pepper
1 onion, sliced
1–2 fresh bay leaves
2–3 sprigs of fresh parsley
150ml malt vinegar

To serve
Mixed green salad

A rather old-fashioned way to serve herrings, let's hope this delicious option will come back into fashion. They keep well in the fridge and make a tasty snack with bread or served on a bed of seasonal salad.

- Preheat the oven to 180°C/gas 4.

- Season the fish, then roll up each fillet and secure with a cocktail stick. Place in a non-metallic, ovenproof dish.

- Add the onion and the herbs. Pour the vinegar over the fish. Cover with foil and pour in enough water to cover the fish.

- Bake in a the oven for 40–45 minutes or until the fish is just tender.

- Leave to cool in the cooking liquid, then discard the bay leaves and peppercorns.

- Serve with salad.

Pepper and Rollmop Salad

A colourful dish made out of Spanish-style ingredients, using different coloured peppers makes for a vibrant-looking salad – plus it tastes good too. Do make sure the rollmops are well drained.

- Trim and thinly slice the fennel bulb, reserving the fronds for garnishing.

- Arrange all the green salad ingredients in a bowl and toss well before adding the sliced rollmops.

- Put all the salad dressing ingredients into a screw-topped jar and shake until evenly mixed together. Pour the sauce into a jug.

- Garnish the salad with the fennel fronds and serve with the dressing.

1 small fennel bulb
1 small red pepper, sliced
1 small green pepper, sliced
1 small yellow pepper, sliced
1 round lettuce
½ cucumber, sliced
1 packet of watercress
2 rollmop herrings (page 50), well drained and sliced into 2.5cm pieces

For the chilli pepper dressing
½ small green chilli pepper, deseeded and very finely chopped
1 garlic clove, crushed
1 tsp sugar
Salt and freshly ground black pepper
1 tbsp lemon juice
4 tbsp olive oil

Soused Herrings

150ml white wine vinegar
150ml white dry wine
150ml water
1 tbsp pickling spice
10 peppercorns
1 bay leaf
1 onion, thinly sliced
1 tbsp sugar
6 boned herrings

Herrings are cheap to buy and rich in omega 3. Ask your fishmonger to bone them for you as it only takes an expert a few minutes to do so. This method of cooking has been used for centuries to preserve fish.

- Put all the ingredients except the fish into a pan. Bring to the boil, then take off the heat and allow to cool.

- Preheat the oven to 160°C/gas 3.

- Place the herring in a large non-metallic bowl and pour over the cooking liquor.

- Cover and cook in the oven for 1 hour.

- Take out of the oven and allow to cool overnight in the fridge.

- Serve with crusty bread and crisp salad.

Avocado Smoked Trout

SERVES 4–6

Serve this recipe as a light lunch, a snack or even as a starter. It is delicious served with sliced rye bread, as it offers a lovely flavour and texture contrast. You can also make this recipe from smoked salmon pieces.

- Cut the avocados in half lengthways, carefully remove the stone and peel them. Slice the flesh into even sized slices and toss in the lemon juice.

- Arrange the trout and avocado on serving plates.

- In a bowl, mix together tarragon, crème fraîche or yoghurt and capers. Season with freshly ground black pepper.

- Drizzle the sauce over the trout and avocado and serve with slices of rye bread.

2 ripe avocados
Juice of ½ lemon
250g smoked trout
1 tsp chopped fresh
tarragon or ½ tsp
dried tarragon
4 tbsp crème fraîche or
10% fat Greek yoghurt
1 tbsp small capers in
sherry vinegar, drained
Freshly ground black
pepper

To serve
Rye bread

Herby Ocean Terrine

675g Scottish farmed
  salmon, skinned and
  roughly chopped
1 tbsp tomato purée
2 tbsp fresh lemon juice
¼ tsp freshly grated
  nutmeg (optional)
300ml crème fraîche
Salt and freshly ground
  black pepper
2 egg whites

For the herb layer
350g white fish, skinned
  and roughly chopped
½ bunch of watercress,
  washed and dried well
1 tsp chopped fresh dill
1 tbsp fresh lemon juice
150ml crème fraîche

To serve
Melba Toast (page 154)
Seasonal salad

Making a terrine is a great way of using off-cuts of fish, allowing for plenty of variety in your choice of ingredients. Serve it in thick slices with freshly made melba toast and a bowl of seasonal salad.

- Preheat the oven to 160°C/gas 3 and lightly grease and line a 1.2 litre loaf tin.

- Place the salmon in a food processor or blender with the tomato purée, lemon juice, nutmeg and crème fraîche. Season, then process until smooth.

- In a clean bowl, whisk the egg whites until stiff. Transfer the salmon mixture to another bowl, then carefully fold in half the egg whites.

- Place the white fish, watercress, dill, lemon juice and crème fraîche in a food processor. Season, then process until smooth.

- Transfer the white fish mixture to a bowl and carefully fold in the remaining egg white.

- Spoon half the salmon mixture into the prepared tin and smooth over the surface. Spoon the herb layer on top, then spoon the remaining salmon mixture over to form the final layer. Smooth the surface.

- Bake in the oven for 1 hour or until firm. Remove and leave to cool.

- Serve in slices with melba toast and salad leaves.

Devonshire Crab Salad

1 tbsp mayonnaise
(page 143)
1 tbsp lemon juice
1 tbsp thick natural
yoghurt
Salt and freshly ground
black pepper
225g crab meat, thawed
if frozen
½ cucumber, diced or
sliced
4–6 cherry tomatoes,
halved
50–75g cooked pasta
shells
2 little gem lettuces,
shredded

To garnish
Ribbons of cucumber
made with a vegetable
peeler
1 lemon, cut into wedges

Ideally buy crabs that have been cooked that day and feel heavy in weight for their size. If you use frozen crabmeat, make sure it is thawed thoroughly. This recipe is ideal for using up leftover cooked pasta.

- In a bowl, mix together the mayonnaise, lemon juice and yoghurt. Season to taste.

- Fold in the crab meat, cucumber, tomatoes and pasta shells, tossing them gently.

- Serve on a bed of shredded lettuce, garnished with cucumber and lemon wedges.

Fishy Tabbouleh

Couscous is a great standby as it can so quickly be transformed into delicious salads or sides dishes. It is worth keeping a packet in your store cupboard. You can also serve this dish with a salad if you like.

- Put the couscous into a large bowl and pour over 450ml boiling water. Stir, cover with clingfilm and leave for 5 minutes, then fluff up with a fork.

- Drain the fish, reserving the oil. Flake the fish with a fork and mix into the couscous with the chickpeas, tomatoes and cucumber.

- To make a simple dressing, mix the reserved fish oil with the lemon juice and mint. Season to taste.

200g couscous
2 x 200g cans of fish like mackerel, tuna, salmon etc.
410g can of chickpeas, drained and rinsed
300g baby plum or cherry tomatoes, halved
½ cucumber, cut into batons
Juice of 1 small lemon
3 tbsp chopped fresh mint
Salt and freshly ground black pepper

Herby Salmon

200g caster sugar
130g sea salt flakes
About 3 tbsp fresh
   horseradish, peeled
   and grated
2 raw beetroots, grated
25g packet of dill,
   reserving a little for
   garnishing
2 salmon fillets, with
   the skin on

For the dressing
225g crème fraîche
Juice of 1 lemon

This is a very colourful and tasty way of serving salmon fillets, yet it is one of the oldest ways of preserving food. Make sure you make this dish with fresh fish rather than fish that has been thawed from frozen. Serve it with fresh, crisp salad.

- In a bowl, mix together the sugar, salt, 2 tsp of the horseradish, the beetroot and dill.

- Line a non-metallic bowl with clingfilm. Spoon half the mixture on to the clingfilm. Lay one fillet skin-side down on the cure, then spoon in the remaining mixture and place the remaining fillet on top skin-side uppermost. Wrap tightly in the clingfilm.

- Put the parcel into a flat dish and weigh it down with a heavy baking tray. Leave the salmon in the fridge for 2–5 days.

- Pour away any liquid, turn the salmon over and weigh down again.

- When you are ready to serve, unwrap the clingfilm and brush off the marinade. Cut the salmon into thin slivers.

- To make the dressing, mix the crème fraîche and lemon juice.

- Serve the salmon and dressing with Melba toast.

To vary
Use fresh salmon or salmon trout fillets.

CHAPTER 4

Hot Lunches and Suppers

Because fish has such a delicate flesh, it cooks quickly by all kinds of methods, so is perfect for everyday cooking in our busy lives. Ideally, use the freshest fish you can buy and use it on the same day. But for many of us that's not possible, so there's no need to ignore frozen options as you can still make nutritious and delicious seafood meals for lunch or supper.

Seafood Jambalaya

Many supermarkets now sell either fresh or frozen ready-prepared seafood, which makes a dish like this simplicity itself. All you need to do is just stir the fish mixture into cooked rice or pasta for a quick treat.

- Heat the oil in a large, heavy-based frying pan or wok, add the onion and garlic and fry for about 4 minutes until soft, stirring frequently.

- Add the pepper and celery and fry for a further 2 minutes.

- Add the rice and stir until the grains are coated with oil.

- Add the tomatoes, white wine, thyme, three-quarters of the stock and the pepper sauce. Bring to the boil, then lower the heat and simmer gently for 15 minutes or until the rice is cooked, stirring occasionally. Add the remaining stock if necessary.

- Stir in all the seafood except the mussels. Cover the pan with a lid and cook for 5 minutes or until the prawns and scallops are just cooked.

- Add the mussels, cover and cook for 3 minutes until the mussels open; discard any that remain closed. Season to taste, then serve piping hot.

2 tbsp rapeseed oil
1 large onion, finely sliced
1 garlic clove, crushed
1 green pepper, deseeded, halved and sliced
2 celery sticks
175g long-grain rice
220g can tomatoes
1 glass dry white wine
1 tsp dried thyme
350ml Fish Stock (page 142)
Dash of pepper sauce
450g mixed seafood like prawns, queen scallops, sliced squid, mussels, uncooked, cleaned
Salt and freshly ground black pepper

Seafood Risotto

5 tbsp rapeseed oil
1 onion, chopped
3 garlic cloves, crushed
225g Arborio rice
100ml dry white wine
1.5 litres Fish Stock
   (page 142)
350g frozen seafood mix,
   thawed
Finely grated zest of 1
   lemon
2 tbsp sun-dried tomatoes,
   finely chopped
1 tbsp chopped fresh
   tarragon
Salt and freshly ground
   black pepper

Use Arborio rice, or risotto rice, for an authentic dish. This is a classic Italian-style dish with a creamy texture. For convenience, you can use ready-prepared mixed frozen seafood, or add extra ingredients like fresh cleaned mussels and clams or squid.

- Preheat a frying pan, add the oil, onion and garlic and cook for about 3 minutes until softened.

- Add the rice and stir until it is hot and shining.

- Pour in the wine and stir until it is absorbed.

- Add 150ml of the stock and stir constantly until the liquid has been absorbed by the rice. Slowly add the remaining stock a little at a time, stirring regularly, for about 10 minutes until the rice is half cooked.

- Stir in the seafood and cook for 4–5 minutes, gradually adding the remaining stock as before until the rice is *al dente*, or just tender to the bite.

- Stir in the lemon zest, tomatoes and tarragon. Remove from the heat, cover and leave for 10 minutes. Serve hot.

Stir-fried Lettuce and Prawns

SERVES 3–4

Quickly stir-fried, lettuce makes an interesting complement to prawns, here cooked with a hint of oriental flavouring to make an economical dish for all the family to enjoy mid week. You could replace the prawns with seafood cocktail.

- Heat the oil in a large frying pan or a wok and stir-fry the onions for 1–2 minutes.

- Add the ginger and prawns and cook for 1 minute.

- Separate the lettuce into leaves and add to the pan with the sherry. Season to taste. Stir quickly for 1–2 minutes then serve at once.

3 tbsp rapeseed oil
1 bunch of spring onions, cut into 5cm pieces
2.5cm piece of root ginger, grated
150g peeled prawns, (thawed if frozen)
1 large crisp lettuce, such as cos, separated into leaves
1 tbsp dry sherry
Salt and freshly ground black pepper

Moules Marinières

2kg fresh large mussels
40g butter
1 onion, thinly sliced
2 garlic cloves, crushed
300ml dry white wine
1 bay leaf
3 tbsp chopped fresh
    flatleaf parsley
Salt and freshly ground
    black pepper
1 tbsp plain flour

To serve
Warm garlic bread

Ideally buy the mussels 24 hours in advance, wash them and place in icy water sprinkled with 3 tbsp of flour. Leave in the base of the fridge overnight, then rinse and drain. This helps to get rid of grit. Serve this as a lunch dish or a starter for 4 people.

- Scrub and beard the mussels in cold running water. Discard any that are broken or remain open.

- Melt half the butter in a large pan and gently sauté the onion for about 3 minutes until just soft but not coloured.

- Add the garlic, dry white wine, bay leaf, half the parsley and season to taste. Add the mussels, cover and bring to the boil. Cook for 2–4 minutes until the mussels are open. Discard any that remain closed. Do not overcook the mussels otherwise they become tough. Discard the bay leaf.

- Using a slotted spoon, lift the mussels into warm serving bowls.

- Heat the cooking liquor. Blend together the flour with the remaining butter, then whisk it into the sauce. Simmer until it thickens slightly, then stir in the remaining parsley. Simmer until the sauce has reduced by one-third, then pour it over the mussels.

- Serve with warmed garlic bread.

To vary
While sautéing the onion, add 50–75g smoky bacon lardons to give the sauce a smoky flavour. You may need to add less seasoning.

Devilled Crab

4 small dressed crabs
50g can of anchovy fillets,
    drained
1 tsp curry powder, mild
or hot
Pinch of cayenne pepper
2 tsp Worcestershire sauce
75g butter
75g soft white
    breadcrumbs

To garnish
A few anchovy fillets
A few sprigs of fresh
    flatleaf parsley

Dressed crabs are readily available in most major supermarkets but not nearly so tasty as this spiced-up variation. If you are using frozen crabs, make sure they are thawed out thoroughly before using. Use mild or hot curry powder, as you wish.

- Preheat the oven to 200°C/gas 6.

- Remove the flesh from the crab shells, wash the shells in cold water and dry well. Blend the light and dark meat together.

- Chop enough anchovy fillets to give 2 tbsp, then mix with the crab meat, curry powder, cayenne pepper and Worcestershire sauce.

- Heat the butter in a frying pan, add the crumbs and cook gently for 1 minute or until crisp and golden brown.

- Add one-third of the crisp breadcrumbs to the crab mixture and stir together. Spoon the fish mixture back into the shells, then top with the remaining buttered crumbs.

- Cook in the oven for 15 minutes or until piping hot and golden brown.

- Serve immediately, garnished with thin strips of anchovy fillets and parsley sprigs.

To vary

Use frozen or canned crab meat instead of fresh, and spoon the mixture into scallop shells or individual ovenproof dishes.

To make Devilled Crab and Avocados, use the crab mixture to fill 3–4 large, halved avocados to make a tasty starter. Simply halve the avocados, and remove and discard the stones. Brush the surfaces with a little oil and lemon juice. Spoon the filling on top and add the buttered crumbs, as described in the recipe. Cook as in the recipe for 10–12 minutes only, as overheated avocados tend to develop a bitter taste.

Prawns in Sleeping Bags

This is a great recipe to serve when entertaining as the stuffed baby squid tubes can be prepared well in advance. The squid acts as a sleeping bag, with the other seafood neatly tucked inside. Make sure you don't overcook them otherwise they'll be tough.

For the sauce
3 cardamom pods, cracked
5cm piece of vanilla pod
1 litre fresh orange juice
180g caster sugar
2 garlic cloves, crushed with the skin on
Salt and freshly ground black pepper

For the squid
12 baby squid tubes, with the tentacles inside
12 large raw tiger prawns, with heads on and the remaining shell off
12 baby asparagus spears
12 small basil leaves
12 cherry tomatoes
12 wooden skewers, soaked in cold water
A little rapeseed oil, for frying
2 garlic cloves, crushed
3 sprigs of fresh thyme

To serve
Baby salad leaves

- Preheat a heavy-based pan and dry-fry the cardamom and vanilla for 1 minute.

- Add the remaining sauce ingredients, bring to the boil, then simmer for 5 minutes to reduce down to one-third and create a thick glaze. Adjust the seasoning to taste. Leave to cool.

- Rinse and pat dry the squid and the tentacles. Stuff the prawns, asparagus, basil leaves and cherry tomatoes into the cavity.

- Thread the contents of the squid securely on to soaked wooden skewers, then add the tentacles and cherry tomatoes. Season to taste.

- Heat the oil in a frying pan and fry the garlic and thyme for 2 minutes.

- Add the squid and cook on each side for 4–5 minutes or until just tender.

- Serve with baby salad leaves and the orange sauce.

To vary
Before stuffing the squid, add about 1 tsp smoked cooked pancetta to each tube. For a smoked effect, just sprinkle over a very little smoked ground paprika.

French-style Prawns in Provençal Sauce

300g brown basmati rice, rinsed
1.3 litres water
200g frozen peas
2 tbsp olive oil
3 shallots, chopped
2 garlic cloves, crushed
1 green pepper, deseeded, halved and sliced
1 yellow pepper, deseeded, halved and sliced
400g can of chopped tomatoes
300ml Fish Stock (page 142)
2 tsp dried *herbes de Provence*
2 tsp tomato purée
Pinch of sugar
300g frozen raw prawns, defrosted
2 tsp cornflour
2 tbsp water

A delicious way to serve frozen prawns in a typical south of France way, this dish has a sauce made from peppers and onions with *herbes de Provence*, a traditional combination usually made up of savory, fennel, basil and thyme.

- Put the rice and water in a large pan and bring to the boil. Cover and simmer for 15 minutes.

- Add the peas, bring back to the boil, then simmer for about 5 minutes or until the rice is *al dente*.

- Meanwhile, heat the oil in a large frying pan and cook the shallots for about 5 minutes until soft but not coloured.

- Add the garlic and cook for 2–3 minutes, then add the peppers and cook for a further 6–8 minutes until softened.

- Pour in the tomatoes, stock, herbs, tomato purée and a little sugar to taste and simmer, uncovered, for 15 minutes.

- Stir in the prawns and bring to a simmer.

- Mix together the cornflour and water, then stir it into the sauce, bring to the boil and stir for a few minutes until the sauce is thickened and the prawns are pink.

- Drain the rice and serve with the prawns.

Mussels with Garlic

This is a simple but tasty dish to make and good to eat too. If you have time, soak the mussels in iced water and flour, as described on page 64, before you prepare them as this helps to remove any ingested grit in the mussels. It serves 4 as a starter.

- Scrub and beard the mussels in cold running water. Discard any that are broken or remain open.

- Melt the butter in a very large pan and add the garlic and shallot. Sauté for 3–4 minutes without browning the garlic.

- Add the mussels, bay leaves, parsley and white wine. Cover and shake the pan occasionally for a few minutes until the mussels have opened; discard any that remain closed. Discard the bay leaves.

- Transfer the mussels to serving bowls using a slotted spoon.

- Bring the juices in the pan to the boil and simmer for a few minutes until reduced by one-third. Season to taste and sprinkle with the parsley.

- Pour the sauce over the mussels and serve at once.

SERVES 2

2–3 tbsp plain flour
A little ice
2kg fresh mussels
100g butter
3 large garlic cloves, chopped
1 banana shallot, finely chopped
2 bay leaves
6 sprigs of fresh flat leaf parsley
150ml dry white wine

To serve
3 tbsp coarsely chopped fresh flatleaf parsley

Stir-fried Scallops

450g frozen scallops,
thawed
2 tsp cornflour
3 tsp sesame oil
300g raw tiger prawns,
peeled
250g sugar snap peas
2 garlic cloves, crushed
2 tsp grated ginger root
150g oyster mushrooms,
wiped
2 bunches of spring
onions, cut into 5cm
pieces
4 small pak choi
Juice of 2 limes
2 tbsp chopped fresh
coriander

To serve
Wild rice

A really versatile dish, this makes a fabulous main meal, or you can serve it as a starter for 8. If you serve it with wild rice, you have a lovely contrast of flavours and textures to enjoy in this oriental-inspired dish.

- Remove the orange coral from the scallops, if attached. Clean the scallops and pat dry. Put the corals into a bowl and mix in the cornflour and 2 tsp sesame oil, stirring well.

- Heat a wok or heavy-based frying pan, add the scallops, corals and prawns, and stir-fry for 3–4 minutes or until just starting to go golden in colour.

- Remove from the pan add the remaining sesame oil. Add the peas, garlic, ginger and oyster mushrooms and stir-fry for 2–3 minutes.

- Add the spring onions and cook for a further minute or so.

- Return the scallops, corals and prawns to the pan and stir together.

- Add the pak choi and cook for a further 1 minute.

- Stir in the lime juice and coriander and cook for 1 more minute.

- Serve with wild rice.

Seared Scallops with Spring Onions

The taste of freshly cooked scallops is wonderful, just make sure that they are not overcooked. Always try to buy scallops collected by hand; they cost a little more than the ones dredged from our seas and they are better for the environment.

- Preheat the oven to 230°C/gas 8.

- Arrange the springs onions and asparagus in a single layer on a heatproof serving dish. Sprinkle over 3 tbsp of the oil and cook in the oven for 3–4 minutes.

- Pat the scallops dry with kitchen paper, then use a sharp knife to score them in a criss-cross pattern.

- Heat the remaining oil in a griddle pan and cook the scallops for 1–2 minutes on each side or until golden brown.

- Remove the vegetables from the oven and arrange evenly on serving plates, then arrange the scallops on top. Serve garnished with snipped chives and lemon wedges.

4 spring onions, halved lengthways then sliced crossways
8 asparagus, trimmed and halved lengthways
4 tbsp rapeseed oil
16 scallops, with or without corals
Salt and freshly ground black pepper

To garnish
1 tbsp snipped fresh chives
1 lemon, cut into wedges or a generous squeeze of lemon juice

Citrus Squid

12 small squid, thawed if
    frozen
Juice of 1 large lemon
2 tbsp olive oil
1 tbsp finely chopped
    fresh lemon thyme
Salt and freshly ground
    black pepper

The secret to cooking squid is not to overcook it otherwise it becomes tough and very chewy. In this recipe, the squid is marinated in lemon juice and herbs, then quickly flash-fried for tender results.

- Wash and clean the squid and remove any tentacles. Cut in half lengthways and score each half with a sharp knife to form diamond shapes, being careful not to cut all the way through the flesh. Place in a non-metallic bowl.

- Mix the lemon juice, oil, thyme, and seasoning in a bowl and pour over the squid. Cover and chill in the fridge overnight.

- When ready to cook, preheat a heavy-based frying pan and cook the squid for about ½–1 minute each side.

> **To vary**
> If your squid came with the tentacles, just clean them and marinate and cook them with the rest of the squid. This recipe is also good cooked over a barbecue.

Salt and Pepper Squid

This simple starter is so good to eat with freshly made aioli used as a dipping sauce. A few lemon wedges will always enhance pretty much any seafood dish, and this is no exception. Cook the tentacles with the body of the squid.

- Rinse the squid under running water and pat dry with kitchen paper.

- Put the seasoned flour into a polythene bag with the prepared squid and shake well until it is lightly coated.

- Fill a deep-fat fryer or large, heavy-based pan one-third full of oil. Heat to 190°C or until a cube of bread turns golden brown in 30 seconds. Fry the squid for 1–2 minutes in batches, keeping it warm while frying the remaining squid. Drain on crumpled kitchen paper.

- Serve piping hot with lemon wedges and aioli dipping sauce.

450g prepared squid, thawed if frozen, cut into 1cm slices
Seasoned plain flour, for dusting
Rapeseed oil, for deep-fat frying

To serve
1 lemon, cut into wedges
Aioli (page 144)

Chunky Fish and Citrus Burger

Children love burgers, especially with chips, so make this for a mid-week meal with any white fish you like: cod, coley, cobbler or haddock, for example. You might like to accompany it with salad or perhaps mushy peas.

400g white fish, skinned and finely chopped
4 tbsp finely chopped fresh parsley
4 tsp capers, rinsed and drained well
Finely grated zest of 1 lemon
A little plain flour
3–4 tbsp olive oil
4 burger buns
180g baby leaf salad
4 tsp tartare sauce

- Place the white fish in a food processor and pulse to a chunky paste. Mix the fish with the parsley, capers and lemon zest. Squeeze the mixture together well, then with floured hands shape into 4 even-sized burger shapes.

- Heat the oil in a heavy-based frying pan. Cook the burger for 4–5 minutes on each side until golden brown and firm to the touch.

- Serve in the buns with the baby lettuce leaves along with the tartare sauce.

Fritto Fish of the Sea

This is poplar in my house: a selection of seafood fried until crisp and golden on the outside and soft and succulent on the inside. A very economical dish, serve it with a crispy colourful seasonal salad. You can also serve it as a starter for 8 guests.

- Sift the flour into a bowl and season liberally.

- Toss all the seafood in the flour until lightly coated, then shake off any excess.

- Heat enough oil in a large saucepan to 180°C, then carefully add a quarter of the coated fish and fry for 2–3 minutes or until crisp and golden brown.

- Remove with a slotted spoon and drain thoroughly on kitchen paper. Keep the fish warm whilst repeating with the remaining fish.

- Garnish with the lemon and parsley and serve immediately.

75g plain flour
Salt and freshly ground
 black pepper
225g pack ready-prepared
 seafood cocktail,
 drained well
225g skinless pollock,
 haddock or cod, cut into
 strips
12 large peeled prawns
 with tail intact
Vegetable oil, for shallow
 frying

To garnish
1 lemon, cut into wedges
A few sprigs of fresh
 flatleaf parsley

Fish Boulangère

500g old potatoes,
  scrubbed well and skins
  left on
Salt and freshly ground
  black pepper
50g butter
1 garlic clove, crushed
750g white fish fillets,
  skinned and cut into
  even-sized pieces
1 large onion, thinly sliced
200ml Fish Stock (page 142)
  or milk

To garnish
1 tbsp finely chopped fresh
  parsley

To serve
Fresh green vegetables

With its layers of fish, onion and thinly sliced potatoes, this makes a tasty supper or lunch dish to serve with peas, green beans or broccoli to bring some colour and texture to your plate. A good mid-week meal for the family that's inexpensive too.

- Preheat the oven to 180°C/gas 4.

- Par boil the potatoes in boiling salted water for 10 minutes. Drain and leave to cool, Then slice thinly.

- Cream half the butter with the garlic and spread over the base of a casserole dish. Put the fish pieces evenly on top and sprinkle with salt and pepper. Cover with the onions and then the potato slices. Pour over the liquid, then dot with the remaining butter.

- Cook in a the oven for 40–50 minutes or until the fish and potatoes are cooked and tender.

- Garnish with the parsley and serve with fresh green vegetables.

Home-made Fish Cakes

Home-made fish cakes are so delicious to eat with a wonderful texture from the fish and a floury potato like Maris Piper. Served with home-made tartare sauce – what could be better? You can use leftover mashed potato if you have any.

- In a bowl, mix together the fish, potato, butter, parsley, seasoning and pepper sauce. Using lightly floured hands, gently knead the mixture together to form a ball. Divide the mixture into 8 even-shaped rounds.

- Coat the cakes with the egg, then the breadcrumbs.

- Heat a little oil in a frying pan, add the fish cakes and fry on one side for about 8–10 minutes until golden brown, then turn and cook until golden and crisp on the other side. Drain on crumpled kitchen paper.

- Serve with seasonal vegetables.

To vary
Add one of the following to the basic mix of potato and fish:
2 shelled and chopped hard-boiled eggs;
75g Cheddar cheese, grated;
4 spring onions, finely shredded;
50g peeled prawns, roughly chopped.

350g cooked fish like pollock, coley, haddock herrings or whiting
350g cooked potato, mashed or put through a ricer
25g unsalted butter
2 tsp finely chopped fresh curly leaf parsley
Salt and freshly ground black pepper
A few drops pepper sauce or Tabasco sauce
A little plain flour
A little egg, to bind
150g fresh fine breadcrumbs
Oil, for shallow-frying

To serve
Seasonal vegetables

Fish Potato Pie

400g white fish, skinned and boned, cut into even-sized pieces
550ml whole milk
50g butter
3–4 tbsp plain flour
Salt and freshly ground black pepper
¼ tsp ready-made English mustard
A little freshly grated nutmeg
150g strong Cheddar cheese, grated
650g cooked mashed potato
3 tomatoes, sliced

A cheesy mashed potato, light and creamy, makes a mouth-watering topping for this traditional fish pie made with any white fish, either one type or a selection of different fish if you prefer.

- Preheat the oven to 150°C/gas 2 and grease an ovenproof dish.

- Put the fish and milk in a pan, bring to a simmer, then simmer gently for about 6 minutes until cooked. Lift the fish out of the milk.

- In a separate pan, melt the butter, then stir in the flour and cook for 2 minutes over a medium heat, stirring continuously. Slowly whisk in the poaching milk, whisking all the time, until you have a smooth sauce. Season to taste, adding a little nutmeg and mustard. Stir in 100g of the cheese. Finally, flake the fish into the cheese sauce.

- Layer half the potato into the base of the prepared dish, top with half the fish in cheese sauce, then the sliced tomatoes. Continue with the remaining fish in cheese sauce, then the remaining potatoes. Sprinkle over the remaining grated cheese.

- Bake in the oven for about 30–40 minutes or until golden brown.

To vary
Add a chopped hard-boiled egg or some crisply fried bacon lardons to the cheese sauce.

White Fish Hot Pot

2 tbsp rapeseed oil
100g green beans
1 courgette, sliced
2 garlic cloves, crushed
100g button mushrooms,
　wiped and sliced
150ml white wine
300ml Fish Stock
　(page 142)
400g can of chopped
　tomatoes
425g can of flageolet
　beans, drained
700g pollock, skinned and
　boned
Salt and freshly ground
　black pepper
1 tbsp dried oregano

To serve
Hot crusty bread

This is an all-in-one recipe that only takes a short time to prepare and 15 minutes to cook. With vegetables, beans and fish in one dish, you don't need anything else to accompany it.

● Heat the oil in a large pan, then add the beans, courgette, garlic and button mushrooms and fry for 2–3 minutes, stirring frequently.

● Pour in the white wine and bring the mixture to the boil, then reduce the heat. Stir in the fish stock and chopped tomatoes and simmer for a few minutes.

● Stir in the flageolet beans and simmer for 5 minutes.

● Add the fish and season to taste. Cover the pan and simmer for a further 5 minutes or until the fish has turned opaque.

● Sprinkle over the oregano and serve with hot crusty bread.

Traditional Fish and Chips

Fish and chips wrapped up in newspaper used to be a Friday-night treat, with an added bonus of mushy peas and a little bag of the small, crispy pieces of batter just like pork scratchings. This batter gives wonderfully light and fluffy results.

- Fill a deep-fat fryer or large, heavy-based saucepan one-third full of oil and heat to 180°C.

- Squeeze the lemon over the cod and season. Dip the fish into the flour and shake off any residue.

- To make the batter, place the remaining flour in a large mixing bowl and whisk in 450ml of the lager. Check that the batter is a good, thick coating consistency. Add a little more lager if it is too gluey, or more flour if it is too thin.

- Cook one fillet at a time. Hold the fish with your finger and thumb, dip in the batter to coat, then shake off any excess. The batter should be thick and coat the fish well.

- Carefully lower the fish into the hot oil and fry for about 5 minutes until crisp and golden. Lift out and drain on crumpled kitchen paper. Keep the fish warm while you fry the remainder.

- Serve with chips and mushy peas.

4 x 225g cod fillets
1 lemon
Salt and freshly ground
    black pepper
250g self-raising flour,
    sifted
600ml lager
Corn or rapeseed oil,
    for deep-fat frying

To garnish
8 sprigs of fresh parsley

To serve
Chunky Chips (page 152)
    or Healthier Chips
    (page 153)
Mushy peas

Simply Grilled Cod with Herb Butter

4 x 175g cod steaks
80g unsalted butter, at
  room temperature,
  plus a little extra
  for greasing
Salt and freshly ground
  black pepper
2–3 garlic cloves, crushed

To garnish
A few sprigs of flat parsley
  or dill

To serve
French beans

Herb butters are easy to make by blending garlic and herbs into some unsalted butter. Use any fish of your choice for this dish, like cobbler, cod or monkfish, and serve it on a stack of freshly cooked French beans.

- Preheat a grill or a griddle pan to a medium heat. Pat the fish dry with kitchen paper.

- Grease pan, then put in the fish. Season well.

- In a bowl, mix together the butter and garlic and spread evenly over the fish. Cook for 7–8 minutes, turning once, or until the fish is just cooked.

- Serve the fish on top of the beans and pour over the garlic butter from the pan. Garnish with fresh herbs.

Baked Cod with Black Olives

Tender cod fillets flavoured with black olives, freshly chopped herbs and a hint of chilli, there is a Provençal feel to this dish. As always with spices, vary the quantity of chilli to suit your own taste.

- Preheat the oven to 230°C/gas 8 and lightly oil a ovenproof baking dish.

- Place the fish fillets in the base of the dish.

- Mix the olives, herbs, spring onions and chillies, spoon on top of the fish and drizzle over the lime juice. Season to taste.

- Bring the tomato juice to the boil in a small pan, then pour around the fish. Place the dish in the oven and cook for 10 minutes or until the fish flakes easily. Serve with a fresh green salad.

1 tbsp vegetable oil
4 x 175g pollock, cod or coley fillets
12 black olives, stoned and sliced
3 tbsp finely chopped fresh parsley
1 tbsp chopped fresh dill
1 bunch of spring onions, thinly sliced
2 red chillies, deseeded and finely chopped
Juice of 2 limes
Salt and freshly ground black pepper
275ml tomato juice

To serve
Fresh green salad

Fish Fillets Veronique

6 small sand dabs or
  3 larger fish
1½ small leeks, trimmed
  and chopped
2 onions, chopped
4 celery sticks, chopped
20 peppercorns
6 tbsp white dry wine
1 small onion, finely diced
350g butter, chilled and
  diced

To garnish
175g muscatel white
  grapes, halved and
  deseeded

You can use dabs or plaice instead of lemon or Dover soles if you prefer. Ask the fishmonger to fillet and bone the fish for you. Don't throw away the bones and white skin but use them to make a homemade fish stock to freeze for future use.

- Preheat the oven to 180°C/gas 4 and lightly grease a flameproof dish.

- Fillet the fish, then fold the fillets in half and season to taste. Place in the prepared dish and set aside.

- Make the stock by washing all the bones and chopping them up to fit into the saucepan. Add enough cold water to cover. Add the leeks, chopped onion, celery, peppercorns and half the white wine and bring quickly to the boil. Reduce the heat and simmer for 15 minutes. Strain and reserve the stock.

- Sprinkle the finely diced onion over the fish, then pour in the remaining white wine and 2 tbsp of the stock.

- Cover with lightly buttered paper and cook in the oven for 8–10 minutes.

- Pass the remaining fish stock through a fine sieve, return to a clean pan and bring to the boil. Boil to reduce the liquid until it coats the back of the spoon. There should be about 150ml.

- Gradually whisk in the butter a piece at a time until melted and well incorporated.

- Pour the sauce over the fish and leave to settle for 2 minutes, then glaze under a hot grill. Arrange the grapes on the serving plates and serve immediately.

Spicy Fish Tagine

3 tsp olive oil
1 large onion, chopped
12 saffron threads
1 tsp ground cumin
750g waxy potatoes, cut
  into 3.5cm chunks
2 celery sticks, chopped
400g can of chopped
  tomatoes
4cm cinnamon stick
275ml water
600g thick cod or haddock
  fillets, cut into 4 cm
  pieces
Salt and freshly ground
  black pepper
2 tbsp chopped fresh
  flatleaf parsley
1–2cm preserved lemon
  (page 98)

To serve
Crusty bread

A tagine is a North African dish and actually
refers to the conical dish in which the recipes
are cooked. This tagine is very filling and spicy
with tart pressed lemons. Serve it with some
chunks of crusty bread.

- In a heavy-based frying pan, heat the olive
  oil and fry the onion, saffron and cumin
  for 4–5 minutes until the onion is golden.

- Add the potatoes, celery, tomato,
  cinnamon and water. Bring to the boil,
  then reduce the heat and simmer for
  10–12 minutes or until the potatoes are
  just soft.

- Add the fish and simmer for a further
  10 minutes.

- Season to taste. Garnish with the parsley
  and preserved lemons, and serve with
  crusty bread.

Hazelnut Fillets of Halibut

Halibut or monkfish are both ideal for this simple recipe. If you want to find a cheaper fish, you will still get great results with something like trout or coley. Ask your fishmonger's advice on the best options.

- Clean the fish and pat dry with kitchen paper.

- Put the nuts on to a plate and press each fillet into the nuts.

- Preheat a griddle pan or grill over a medium heat. Add the fish and cook for 5–6 minutes each side or until the fish is tender and just cooked. Take care not to overcook the fish otherwise it will become tough.

- Transfer the fish to serving plates with any loose nuts from the pan and sprinkle with lemon zest to serve.

75g shelled hazelnuts, lightly toasted and chopped
4 x 200g halibut fillets
50g unsalted butter, melted
1 tsp finely grated lemon zest

Oaty Herrings

4 herrings, cleaned, boned,
   with heads and tails
   removed
Salt and freshly ground
   black pepper
125–150g fine oatmeal or
   fine rolled oats

To garnish
1 lemon, cut into wedges
A few sprigs of fresh
   flatleaf parsley

Herrings are so cheap to buy. Always choose ones that have bright red eyes with a firm flesh and no unpleasant smell. Ask your fishmonger to bone and clean them if you like. Do make sure that they are scaled well before cooking.

- Season the herrings and put the oats on to a plate. Press the herrings into the oats, making sure they are coated well on each side.

- Preheat a grill or a non-stick frying pan.

- Cook the fish under the hot grill for 7–8 minutes, turning once, until they flake.

- Transfer to a warm serving plate and garnish with lemon wedges and parsley to serve.

> **To vary**
> Dip the flattened-out herring in a little eaten egg, then into a mixture of ground almonds and oats for a nutty taste.

Mustardy Mackerel

As an oily fish with a strong flavour, mackerel responds well to feisty sauces, like this combination of a mustard coating and a pepper relish. This recipe works well with other oily fish like herring or some white fish, like cod or pollock.

- Rinse the mackerel and pat dry.

- Mix together the breadcrumbs, mustard, lemon zest and herbs. Coat the fish with the flour, brush with egg, then coat in the breadcrumb mixture.

- Heat 4 tbsp oil in a heavy-based frying pan. Fry the fish for about 5 minutes or until golden, turning once. Drain on kitchen paper and keep warm.

- To make the relish, heat the oil in a pan and fry the onion, pepper and paprika for 5 minutes. Stir in the lemon juice, sweetcorn and cucumber and remove from the heat.

- Garnish the mackerel with slices of lemon and serve with the relish and a seasonal salad.

2 large mackerel, filleted
75g fresh breadcrumbs
½ tsp dry mustard
Grated zest of 1 lemon
1 tsp mixed dried herbs
50g plain flour
1 egg, beaten
Oil, for shallow-frying

For the relish
1 tbsp oil
1 small onion, sliced
1 red pepper, deseeded, finely diced
¼ tsp ground paprika
Juice of 1 lemon
75g canned sweetcorn, drained
¼ cucumber, finely diced

To serve
Slices of lemon
Seasonal salad

Marinated Mackerel

30ml white wine vinegar
Freshly squeezed juice of
1 lemon
Freshly squeezed juice of
1 lime
Salt and freshly ground
black pepper
450g mackerel fillets, with
skin left on
50g butter

To garnish
1 lemon, cut into wedges
Sprigs of fresh flatleaf
coriander

Mackerel tastes delicious when marinated, and this wine and citrus fruit dressing gives great results every time. Do use a non-metallic dish when using lemon or other juices, otherwise the acid can react with the metal.

- In a shallow non-metallic dish, mix together the vinegar, lemon and lime juice and seasoning. Lay the mackerel fillets skin-side uppermost in the marinade and marinate for 2–3 hours.

- Lift the mackerel out of the marinade and place skin-side down on a grill pan lined with foil. Place under a preheated, medium grill for 4–5 minutes, basting frequently with the marinade.

- Meanwhile, melt the butter in a frying pan, add the lemon juices and fry gently for about 5 minutes or until softened. Add the fillets skin-side up and cook for 2 minutes basting frequently.

- Check that the fish is cooked by inserting a fork into the thickest part; it should be opaque all the way through. Transfer to a warmed serving plate. Garnish with lemon wedges and coriander. Serve immediately.

Asian Spicy Fish

This is a quick dish to make, popular in Singapore where it is served as street food – which is among the best! The subtle hint of Asian spices perfectly complements the delicate texture and flavour of the fish.

- Make a quick paste by blending together the chillies, shallots, garlic, lemon grass, ginger, soy sauce and sugar with a hand blender or with a pestle and mortar.

- Heat the oil in a heavy-based frying pan and fry the paste for 1–2 minutes, stirring all the time. Season to taste.

- Place another pan over a medium heat and add the fish. Spoon the sauce over the fish in a thin layer and cook gently for 8–10 minutes or until the fish flakes away easily. Be careful not to overcook the fish.

- Serve with noodles.

2 red chillies, deseeded and chopped
4 shallots, finely chopped
2 garlic cloves
1 stick of fresh lemon grass, remove outer leaves and chop the remaining
3.5cm cube fresh ginger root, peeled and grated
2 tsp soy sauce
Pinch of sugar
Salt and freshly ground black pepper
2 tbsp oil
4 x 160g sole or plaice fillets

To serve
Noodles

Citrus Fish Fingers

500g thick fillet of pollock, haddock or white fish of your choice
30g plain flour seasoned with salt and freshly ground black pepper
1 large egg, beaten
50g naturally dried breadcrumbs
1–2 tbsp rapeseed oil
4 tbsp mayonnaise (page 143)
1 tbsp grated lemon zest
2 tbsp fresh chopped herbs
Freshly ground black pepper, to taste

To garnish
1 fresh lemon or lime, cut into wedges

To serve
Chips and seasonal vegetables

These crispy homemade fish fingers are easy to make and a great catch for all the family. Serve with chips and peas, a dollop of homemade mayonnaise flavoured with lemon and fresh herbs.

- Cut the fish fillets into 6–8 short rectangular fingers.

- Place the seasoned flour, beaten egg and breadcrumbs on separate plates. Dip the fish into the flour, then the egg and lastly the breadcrumbs.

- Heat the oil in a large, heavy-based frying pan over a gentle heat. Cook the fish fingers for 3–4 minutes each side or until golden brown and cooked through.

- Meanwhile, mix the mayonnaise with the lemon zest and herbs. Season to taste with pepper.

- Garnish the fish with lemon or lime wedges and serve with chips and seasonal vegetables.

Spicy Pollock with Lentils

SERVES 4

Another firm fish that is becoming increasingly popular, lentils and spinach make a good complement in flavours and a lovely way of serving pollock. Use a mild or hotter curry paste to suit your own taste.

- Preheat a large frying pan and dry-fry the curry paste for 1 minute.

- Add the lentils and water and bring to a simmer.

- Add the fish skin-side upper most. Cover and cook for 6–8 minutes or until the fish is just cooked.

- Meanwhile, make the dressing by putting the olive oil and lemon juice in a screw-topped jar. Shake well, then season to taste.

- Carefully lift out the fish and keep it warm. Increase the heat under the pan, add the spinach cook for a few minutes until just wilted.

- Spoon the lentil and spinach mixture on to 4 serving plates and top with the fish. Pour the dressing over the fish and serve with a mixed salad.

4 tsp curry paste, mild or hot
400g can ready cooked lentils, drained and rinsed
150ml water
4 x 175g pollock, cod or salmon fillet with skin on
5 tbsp olive oil
Juice of 1 large lemon
100g baby spinach, washed and drained well

To serve
Fresh mixed salad

Spanish Chorizo Pollock Cassoulet

100g smoked bacon
  lardons or streaky
  bacon cut up into
  10mm pieces
1 red onion, chopped
1 green pepper, deseeded,
  thinly sliced
1 garlic clove, crushed
200–225g chorizo, diced
  finely
2 x 410g cans of butter
  beans, drained
300g pollock, cut into
  3.5cm cubes
150ml hot Fish Stock
  (page 142)
12 cherry or plum
  tomatoes

To garnish
2 tbsp chopped fresh
  parsley

A lovely combination of fish, Spanish chorizo sausage, cherry tomatoes and butter beans, this is a strongly flavoured dish that makes a great family favourite. Serve it with chunks of crusty bread.

- Heat a heavy-based pan and cook the lardons over a medium heat for about 5 minutes until crispy and golden. Once cooked, remove from the pan and drain on kitchen paper.

- In the same pan, add the onion, pepper and garlic and fry for 3–4 minutes, then add the chorizo and butter beans. Add the fish and the stock and heat gently for 8–12 minutes or until just cooked.

- Add the tomatoes and lardons and season to taste.

- Serve garnished with the parsley.

Tangy Nutty Pollock

This dish is so quick to make but the sharp tang of the lemon perfectly complements the fish. It makes a lovely summer dish served with a crisp salad, or marry it with mashed potatoes and freshly steamed French beans.

- In a large, heavy-based frying pan, melt the butter until just starting to turn a pale brown colour.

- Add the lemon juice and pine nuts and cook for 1–2 minutes.

- Add the fish and cook for 2–3 minutes each side or until the fish is just cooked.

- Garnish with lemon wedges and serve with a salad or with mashed potatoes on a bed of French beans.

100g unsalted butter
2 tbsp fresh lemon juice
3–4 tbsp pine nuts
4 x 175g white fish fillets, like cod, coley or pollock

To garnish
1 lemon, cut into wedges

To serve
Fresh salad or mashed potato and French beans

Red Mullet with Preserved Lemons

2 lemons
3 tbsp rock salt
2 garlic cloves, crushed
  with a little rock salt
30 black olives, pitted and
  roughly chopped
10g fresh basil leaves,
  roughly chopped
10g fresh flatleaf parsley,
  roughly chopped
Juice of 1 lemon juice
3 tbsp olive oil, plus a
  little extra for basting
Salt and freshly ground
  black pepper
4 x 300g red mullet

To serve
Flatbreads and Greek-style
  salad

This is a dish from the Mediterranean area of North Africa and Turkey, which uses lemons preserved in salt. It is a wonderful dish, best made with the freshest of fish caught and cooked at the seaside.

- Make the preserved lemons by putting the 2 lemons and the rock salt into a small saucepan and just covering with water. Place a small plate on top to keep the lemons submerged. Bring to the boil, then simmer for about 10–12 minutes until soft. Refresh under cold water and leave to cool.

- Preheat the oven to 180°C/gas 4.

- Cut off the zest and white pith, then finely chop the flesh.

- In a bowl, mix the garlic, olives, basil, parsley and preserved lemon flesh. Add the lemon juice and 3tbsp olive oil and season well with freshly ground black pepper.

- Pat the red mullet dry and evenly divide the mixture into the cavity of the mullet.

- Heat a little oil in a frying pan and cook for 2–3 minutes each side, then place in the oven for a further 5 minutes or until cooked and crisp.

- Serve with a Greek-style salad and flat breads.

Pan-fried Salmon with Beetroot Salsa

SERVES 4

This recipe works well with any fried or poached fish, but salmon is my particular favourite so do give this version a try. The flavours of the salmon and beetroot are particularly good with each other.

- Make the salsa first by dicing the beetroot into 5mm pieces and mixing in a bowl with the spring onions, chilli, mint, olive oil and lemon juice to taste. Season to taste.

- Put a little plain flour into a polythene bag and put in the fish. Shake well to evenly coat the fish.

- Melt the butter and oil in a large frying pan and fry the fish for 4–5 minutes on each side until the fish flakes easily.

- Serve hot with the salsa.

For the salsa
350g fresh cooked beetroot
1 bunch of spring onions, thinly sliced
1 green chilli, halved, lengthways, seeded and finely chopped
2 tbsp chopped fresh mint
3 tbsp olive oil
1–2 tbsp lemon juice
Salt and freshly ground black pepper

For the fish
4 x 175g pieces of salmon with skin on
A little plain flour
40g unsalted butter
2 tbsp olive oil

Salmon and Sweet Potato Fish Cakes

500ml good Fish Stock
(page 142)
400g sweet potatoes,
peeled and cut into
bite-sized pieces
250g sustainable salmon,
skinned
Salt and freshly ground
black pepper
2 eggs, lightly beaten
Squeeze of lemon juice
2 tbsp freshly snipped
chives
100g naturally dried
breadcrumbs
A little oil, for shallow
frying

To serve
Seasonal salad or fresh
vegetables

Children love fish cakes, so what a great way to get them to eat a healthy portion of oily fish like salmon. With the added sweetness of the potato, it'll be a real family favourite in no time.

- Put the fish stock into a large pan, bring to the boil, then reduce the heat to a simmer. Add the sweet potatoes to the stock and cook for about 5 minutes.

- Add the fish and continue to simmer for about 10 minutes until the potatoes are tender. Remove from the heat.

- Remove the potatoes from the pan with a slotted spoon and mash them well.

- Lift out the fish, flake the flesh and fold it into the potatoes. Season, and stir in one egg, the lemon juice and chives. Mix well, then cover and put in the fridge to chill well for about 1 hour.

- Divide the mixture into 4 large or 8 small fish cakes. Put the remaining beaten egg in a shallow bowl and the breadcrumbs into another. Dip the cakes into the egg, shaking off any excess, then into the breadcrumbs. Repeat until all the egg and breadcrumbs are used and the fish cakes are well coated.

- Heat the oil and fry the fish cakes for about 10 minutes, turning once, until golden brown.

- Drain on kitchen paper and serve with seasonal salad or fresh vegetables.

To vary
To ring the changes, cut the fish cakes into animal shapes – like a lion, rabbit, dog, etc. – using different large biscuit cutters.

Oriental-style Salmon

600g piece of salmon
fillet with skin on
8 tbsp soy sauce
8 tbsp mirin
4 tbsp sake
2cm piece of fresh root
ginger, cut into
matchsticks

To serve
Thin noodles

A tasty way to serve salmon for all the family, when buying the fish make sure you choose the thick end of the fillet. Many supermarkets offer amazing deals at the weekend, so look out for them when buying salmon.

- Cut the fish into 4 even-sized pieces and place in a shallow, non-metallic dish.

- Mix together the soy sauce, mirin and sake, pour over the fish and leave to marinate for 30 minutes.

- Preheat a heavy-based frying pan until hot. Add the fish skin-side down and cook for about 5 minutes each side until golden brown, turning once and basting with any remaining marinade. Make sure not to overcook the fish.

- Garnish the fish with the strips of ginger on top of each fillet and serve immediately with thin noodles.

To vary
Replace the fish with salmon trout fillets or brown trout fillets

Spicy Sea Bass

SERVES 4

This recipe is quick to make and serve, so ideal for an everyday meal. You could replace the sea bass with John Dory fillets if you like. The fish looks ugly but the flesh is tender, moist and flavoursome.

- Preheat the grill to high.

- In a bowl, mix together the garlic, shallots, chilli and lemon juice.

- Brush the chilli mixture on to the fillets. Place under the grill and cook for 4–7 minutes on each side or until just cooked.

- Serve hot with salad leaves, garlic mayonnaise and baby new potatoes.

4 sea bass fillets, dried well
2 garlic cloves, crushed
2 banana shallots, finely chopped
2 small red chillies, halved, deseeded and finely chopped
Juice of ½ lemon

To serve
Garlic mayonnaise see page 144), salad and baby new potatoes

Skate with Capers

4 skate wings, about
   300–325g
Salt and freshly ground
   black pepper
50g unsalted butter
45g baby capers, drained
   well and 1 tbsp white
   wine vinegar reserved

To serve
Seasonal vegetables

Skate has a lovely delicate flavour with a soft texture, and the added advantage of few bones, so it is a great one to introduce to children to start them expanding their repertoire of foods.

● Put the fish in a large roasting tin and just cover with water. Bring to the boil, then reduce the heat and simmer for 10–15 minutes. Season to taste.

● Meanwhile, melt the butter in a small pan and gently cook until it turns golden in colour. Add the capers and vinegar and continue to cook until the sauce just starts to bubble.

● Drain the fish on kitchen paper and place on hot serving plates. Pour the sauce over the fish and serve with seasonal vegetables.

Mediterranean-style Baked Tilapia

SERVES 4

Tilapia are farmed fish from the tropical seas which can be bought in supermarkets and fishmongers around the UK. The flesh is firm and tasty, and is suitable for all types of cooking.

- Preheat the oven to 180°C/gas 4.

- Heat the oil in a heavy-based frying pan. Add the garlic and onions to the pan and fry for about 2 minutes or until softened. Add the pepper and mushrooms and fry for a further 3 minutes.

- Drain the tomatoes, reserving the juice, and roughly chop the flesh. Stir both flesh and juice into the pan with the wine, olives and parsley. Season to taste. Bring to the boil, then simmer gently for 5 minutes.

- Season the inside of the fish, place in a large, lightly greased ovenproof dish and pour over tomato juice mixture. Cover with lid or foil and bake in the oven for 15–20 minutes or until the fish flakes easily. Serve at once with boiled rice.

30ml olive oil
1 garlic clove, crushed
1 small onion, sliced
1 red onion, sliced
1 green pepper, deseeded, sliced
50g button mushrooms, wiped and sliced
400g can of plum tomatoes
300ml white wine
8 black olives, pitted and halved
1 tbsp chopped fresh parsley
Salt and freshly ground black pepper
4 Jamaican red tilapia or red mullet, gutted and cleaned

To serve
Boiled rice

Tilapia with Coriander Couscous

4 whole tilapia, about
   325g each
3–4 tbsp olive oil
1 onion, finely chopped
2 garlic cloves, crushed
300ml Fish Stock
   (page 142)
100g plain couscous
2 tbsp chopped fresh
   coriander
A little oil, for greasing
50g shelled pistachio or
   cashew nuts
2 tbsp lemon juice
Salt and freshly ground
   black pepper

To garnish
1 lemon, cut into wedges
4 sprigs of fresh coriander

Now easy to obtain in supermarkets and fishmongers in the UK, you can buy tilapia either whole or in fillets; the female is smaller than the male. It used to be known as St Peter's fish. You will need to make sure the fish has been scaled.

- Rinse the fish and dry with kitchen paper.

- Heat 2 tsbp oil the in a pan, and fry the onion over a low heat for 3 minutes, stirring occasionally, until softened.

- Add the garlic and cook for a further 2 minutes.

- Pour in the stock and stir in the couscous and coriander. Bring to the boil, then remove from the heat and eave to stand for 15 minutes or until the liquid has been absorbed.

- Preheat the oven to 200°C/gas 6 and grease a large ovenproof dish.

- Stir the couscous with a fork, then stir in the nuts and lemon juice.

- Season the fish inside and out and place in the prepared dish. Spoon the couscous mixture into the middle of the fish, then drizzle over the remaining oil.

- Bake for 20 minutes or until the fish flakes easily. Serve on a hot plate and garnish with lemon and coriander.

To vary
Replace the herb with herbs of your choice like mint, parsley or young thyme.

Trout in a Parcel

4 trout
1 tbsp rapeseed oil
1 lime or lemon, cut into
    12 wedges
4 sprigs of fresh parsley,
    tarragon or dill
Salt and freshly ground
    black pepper

To serve
Fresh salad leaves
Mayonnaise (page 143)

This recipe is simple to make and ready in no time at all. The trout is cooked in its own juices and can be cooked either in the oven, steamer or simply on a barbecue. Serve the fish with a little freshly made mayonnaise. Leave the head on or remove it, as you prefer.

- Preheat the oven to 190°C/gas 5 or prepare a barbecue.

- Cut out 8 pieces of double thickness foil 30x30cm in size. Put 2 pieces on top of each other. Lightly oil the foil on the top side.

- Open out the trout and clean well with a little table salt to remove any blood. Wash well and pat dry. Put a large sprig of your chosen herbs in the middle and season with salt and pepper. Score the fish 3 times into the thickest part of the flesh. Place the fish on to the oiled foil. Put 3 citrus wedges into each fish. Wrap up each fish tightly to form a neat parcel.

- Place on a baking tray and cook in oven or over the coolest part of the barbecue coals. Cook for about 15–20 minutes or until cooked.

- Carefully unwrap and serve with mayonnaise, fresh salad leaves and a squeeze of the citrus wedges.

To vary
Replace the trout with either mackerel or sea bass.

Trout with Fried Rocket and Sesame

4 x 180g trout or red
   mullet fillets
Vegetable oil, for deep-fat
   frying
1 packet wild rocket,
   rinsed and dried well
1 tbsp olive oil
Salt and freshly ground
   black pepper
25g toasted sesame seeds

To serve
Baby new potatoes

Use boneless fillets for this recipe and make sure that all the scales are removed before cooking. You can use trout or red mullet – both will give you great results. Toasting the sesame seeds in a dry pan before cooking gives them a nutty flavour.

- Take the fillets of fish skin-side uppermost and with a sharp knife make a pretty criss-cross pattern into the skin and flesh.

- Carefully heat the oil in a deep-fry fryer or large, heavy-based saucepan to 180°C.

- Make sure that the rocket is dried well with kitchen paper. Deep-fry the rocket in 2–3 batches for 1–2 minutes until translucent, then drain on kitchen paper. Keep warm whilst cooking the other batches.

- Heat the olive oil in a non-stick pan and cook the fish skin-side down for 2 minutes, then turn and cook the other side. Season the fish well.

- Put the rocket on to serving plates and sprinkle on the sesame seeds. Top with the fish and serve with baby new potatoes.

To vary
Add 1–2 garlic cloves to the pan when cooking the fish.

Mid-week Tuna Hash

Buy canned tuna either in brine, spring water or in oil, whichever you prefer. This is not only a tasty recipe, it is very economical too, so ideal for all the family or for students or others on a tight budget.

- Cook the potatoes in boiling salted water for about 10 minutes or until tender. Drain well and leave to get cold.

- Heat the oil in a large frying pan and sauté the onion until just soft; this takes about 4–5 minutes.

- Add the potatoes and the curry paste, crushing the potatoes roughly as you go with a fork.

- Stir in the tuna and cook for a few minutes until the fish and potatoes start to go brown. Stir in the coriander just before serving.

1½ kg baby new potatoes
2 tbsp oil
2 onions, chopped
2 tbsp curry paste,
    medium or hot
2 x 200g cans of tuna,
    drained and flaked
4 tbsp chopped fresh
    coriander

Tuna with Basil, Olives and Tomato

12 small plum or cherry
tomatoes
12 fresh basil leaves,
roughly torn
50g stoned black olives
2 tbsp white balsamic
vinegar
4 tbsp extra virgin olive
oil
1 tsp rapeseed or light
olive oil
4 x 175g fresh tuna fillets
1 x 150g packet rocket
and pea sprouts

This is one of my favourite dishes, simply served with wild rocket and pea sprouts. Choose dolphin-friendly tuna that has firm, pink flesh, not dark brown in colour, and be careful not to overcook the fish otherwise it becomes tough and dry.

● In a bowl, mix together the tomatoes, basil, olives, white balsamic vinegar and extra virgin olive oil.

● Put the rapeseed in a large, non-stick griddle pan over medium to high heat. Add the tuna fillets and cook on one side for 1–2 minutes.

● Carefully turn over the fillets and reduce the heat to medium. Cook for a further 3–5 minutes.

● Serve on warmed plates with the tomato mixture, and a rocket and pea sprout salad.

Irish-style Jacket Potatoes

An colourful and inexpensive dish to make, the potatoes are filled with a lovely savoury mixture of bacon lardons, shredded cabbage and smoked fish. You can serve it as a complete meal or accompany with a salad.

- Preheat the oven to 200°C/gas 6.

- Prick the potatoes with a fork and cook in the oven for 1–1/2 hours or in the microwave for 13–15 minutes on high setting at 800 watts. Allow to cool.

- Meanwhile, heat a frying pan and cook the bacon for 5–10 minutes until pale golden brown. Add the fish.

- Steam the cabbage for about 4–5 minutes until just cooked, then drain well.

- Cut the top off the potatoes and carefully scoop out the cooked potato into a bowl, leaving the outer shell intact. Mash well with the milk and butter, then fold in all the other ingredients.

- Spoon the potato mixture back into the skins and bake in the oven for a further 15–20 minutes. Serve hot.

4 large baking potatoes like King Edward, washed and dried
150g smoked bacon lardons
250g cooked smoked fish fillets, flaked
6 tbsp milk
50g butter
200g hard green cabbage like savoy, finely shredded
4 spring onions, thinly sliced

Smoked Coley Treat

350g skinned smoked
  pollock or coley
100g fresh beetroot,
  grated
1 large carrot, finely
  shredded
100g white cabbage,
  shredded
2 tsp horseradish sauce
4 tbsp Greek-style natural
  yoghurt
Salt and freshly ground
  black peppercorns
1 ciabatta loaf
A little olive oil
1 tbsp snipped fresh
chives

A quick smoked fish ciabatta, this can be made
from frozen or chilled smoked fish, just make
sure it is fully defrosted. You could use pollock,
coley or another smoked white fish of your
choice.

- Preheat the grill and cook the fish on the
  grill trivet for 12–15 minutes, turning
  once.

- While the fish is cooking, make the sauce
  by mixing together the beetroot, carrot,
  cabbage, horseradish and yoghurt. Season
  to taste.

- Heat a ribbed griddle pan or a grill. Split
  the bread in half lengthways and drizzle
  with a little olive oil. Grill the bread until
  light golden brown.

- Pile the coleslaw on top of each piece of
  bread, then flake the fish on top of the
  bread. Season to taste and sprinkle with
  chives to serve.

Smoked Haddock and Chive Jackets

Choose large, unblemished potatoes weighing about 175g each for this recipe. Look out for Maris Piper, Cyprus, Rousters Reds and Cara potatoes, as these are ideal varieties for baking.

- Preheat the oven to 200°C/gas 6.

- Rub the potatoes with a little oil and then season the skins well with salt and pepper.

- Bake in the oven for 1½ hours or until tender and crispy golden brown.

- In a bowl, mix the haddock and chives together and season to taste with the lemon juice and ground black pepper.

- Cut the top off the potato and scoop out two-thirds of the cooked potato. Mix the scooped out potato with the haddock, then pile back into the potato shells and serve at once.

2 baking potatoes,
   scrubbed and pricked
   with a fork
A little oil
Salt and freshly ground
   black pepper

For the filling
100g smoked haddock,
   cooked and mashed
1 tbsp finely snipped
   chives
A dash of lemon juice

Fish under a Pillow

225g ready rolled puff
pastry, thawed if frozen
1 egg yolk
½ tsp English mustard
225g broccoli, cut into
florets
50ml dry white wine
2 tbsp wholegrain mustard
200ml crème fraîche
250g smoked haddock or
cod
115g uncooked tiger tails
prawns, peeled
50g mushrooms, wiped
and sliced
Salt and freshly ground
black pepper

To garnish
Lemon slices

The secret of this great little dish is to grill the
puff pastry evenly. Give it a try – it really works!
Keep the pastry covered while it is thawing
otherwise it will dry out and go crumbly.

- Preheat the grill to high.

- Lay the pastry on a floured surface and cut
  out 4 large fish shapes, then place them on
  a dampened baking tray. Score the surfaces
  lightly with a sharp knife.

- Mix together the egg yolk and English
  mustard, then brush over the fish shapes.

- Reduce the grill to medium and grill the
  fish shapes for 5–6 minutes or until well
  risen, golden brown and cooked through.
  Keep them warm.

- Meanwhile, bring the pan of water to the
  boil, add the broccoli florets and simmer
  for 3–4 minutes until tender but still
  crunchy. Drain and set aside.

- In a separate pan, bring the wine and wholegrain mustard to a simmer for 5–6 minutes. Spoon in the crème fraîche and mix well, followed by the fish, prawns, mushrooms and broccoli florets. Season to taste.

- Stir gently over a low heat for a further 6–8 minutes without allowing the mixture to boil until all the ingredients are well coated with the sauce and the fish is cooked through.

- Spoon the fish and vegetable mixture on to 4 serving plates top each one with a pastry shape and serve immediately, garnished with lemon slices.

Smoked Haddock Surprise

150ml single cream
225g cooked smoked
  haddock or cod fillets
1 tbsp lemon or lime juice
Salt and freshly ground
  black pepper
4 eggs

To serve
1 tbsp chopped fresh
  parsley
Toast or Melba Toast
  (page 154)

A very tasty, light dish to make that all the family will enjoy. Most smoked haddock in supermarkets is now naturally smoked, so it doesn't have that harsh orange of coloured smoked fish, which is quite unnecessary.

- Preheat the oven to 180°C/gas 4. Lightly grease 4 ramekins and place in the oven whilst heating up.

- Place 1 tbsp cream into each dish, flake the fish and mix with the lemon or lime juice and seasoning, then spoon into the dishes. Break an egg into each dish and top with the remaining cream.

- Stand the dish in a roasting dish and fill with hot water to come halfway up the sides of the dishes. Cover with foil and cook for 13–15 minutes or until the eggs are just set.

- Serve immediately with plain or melba toast and a sprinkling of parsley.

CHAPTER 5

Fish on the Barbecue

With a little care, you can make some delicious fish dishes on the barbecue, as fish lends itself very well to absorbing the smoky flavours. The important thing is not to cook over coals that are too hot, otherwise the fish will dry out or burn, so do keep a watchful eye on the fish whilst cooking.

One way to add flavour and also to tenderise the food is to marinate it before you put it on the barbecue. Marinades for fish are usually based on oil or fruit juice. Fish needs to be marinated for at least 30 minutes in a fridge.

If you cook whole fish – such as mackerel, sardines, trout or salmon – first dip the head, tail and fins in water, then in kitchen salt. This will act as a guard to help preventing overcooking. Then place the fish in a fish holder to prevent the delicate flesh dropping on to the coals.

Firm-fleshed fish can be cut into chunks and threaded on to soaked wooden skewers.

Another option is to wrap the fish in a foil parcel to protect the fish and prevent it from drying out. Once cooked, don't throw away any juices you might find in the parcel as these are perfect for flavouring a sauce to accompany the fish.

Herb-stuffed Sardines

900g fresh sardines,
  gutted and scaled
4 tbsp chopped fresh
  herbs, like mint or
  flatleaf parsley
Grated zest and juice of
  2 large lemons
275ml olive oil
2 large onions, very thinly
  sliced
A little freshly ground
  black pepper

To garnish
1 lemon, cut into wedges
A few sprigs of fresh herbs

To serve
Crusty French bread

Sardines are delicious cooked on the barbecue, but if it's not outdoor weather, they work well cooked under a grill too. The bulk of the sardines caught in British waters are exported to Spain and Portugal but you can still enjoy them at home.

- Wash and dry the sardines well.

- In a bowl, mix together the herbs, lemon zest and juice, oil and onions. Season with the ground pepper.

- Cook the fish on a preheated barbecue or under a preheated grill for 2–3 minutes each side, basting with the olive oil mixture.

- Garnish with the lemons and herbs and serve hot with the dressing on the side and chunks of crusty French bread. Alternatively, leave to cool and serve at room temperature.

Tarragon-basted Salmon and Prawns

You can use any firm-fleshed, sustainable fish instead of the salmon in this recipe so try it out with some of your favourites. You can also try different herbs instead of tarragon – perhaps dill or parsley.

- In a screw-topped jar, combine the wine, lemon juice, oil, garlic, tarragon and seasoning. Put on the lid and shake well to mix.

- Cut the salmon into 16 equal 2.5cm cubes, then place in a shallow dish and pour over the marinade. Chill for 30 minutes.

- Remove the salmon from the marinade and thread on to skewers alternately with the prawns and lemon wedges.

- Cook on a preheated barbecue for 8–10 minutes, basting and turning frequently, for about 10 minutes until the fish flakes easily. Then serve immediately.

150ml dry white wine
Freshly squeezed juice
  of 1 lemon
3 tbsp olive or rapeseed
  oil
1 garlic clove, crushed
1 tbsp chopped fresh
  tarragon
Salt and freshly ground
  black pepper
675g farmed salmon
  fillet
16 headless prawns
2 lemons, cut into
  wedges

Barbecued Sardines with Pan-fried Rosemary

8 whole sardines, cleaned and scaled and rinsed well.
2 tbsp sunflower or rapeseed oil
12 small young sprigs of fresh rosemary
Salt and freshly ground black pepper

To garnish
1 lime, cut into 8 wedges

To serve
Pitta bread

Strictly speaking, sardines are young pilchards. sprats or herrings. They are ideal for canning in brine, oil and tomato sauce. The best time of year to catch them is November to April.

- Rinse the sardines under running water, then pat dry with kitchen paper.

- Brush the sardines with the oil. Place two sprigs of rosemary into the middle of each fish and season lightly.

- Wrap the sardines in foil and place on the barbecue for 2–3 minutes each side or until the sardines are golden brown, but do not overcook as they will fall apart.

- Alternatively, place them in a griddle pan or frying pan and fry until cooked.

- Garnish with the lime wedges and serve with pitta bread.

To vary
Try cooking the fish in a fish cage over a preheated barbecue for the same length time. To spice up the oil, add a few drops of a pepper sauce.

Chunky Fish Kebabs

These are quick to make and very tasty – the flavour will benefit from a longer marinating time so leave them as long as possible. Try an assortment of fish or just use one variety.

- Mix the marinade ingredients together in a non-metallic bowl.

- Wash and dry the fish and cut into 3cm pieces.

- Add the fish to the marinade and stir gently until the fish is coated. Cover with clingfilm and leave for 2 hours, stirring once or twice.

- Blanch the shallots boiling water for 2 minutes, then drain.

- Thread the fish, courgettes, pepper, tomatoes and drained shallots on to 4 oiled metal skewers or 4 soaked wooden ones.

- Brush with the remaining marinade and barbecue or grill for 4–5 minutes each side or until the fish is firm and just cooked. Baste them when turning the kebabs over.

- Serve hot with lemon wedges and pitta bread

For the marinade
8 tbsp oil
2 tbsp runny honey
Grated zest of 1 and
    juice of 2 lemons
2 bay leaves, crumbled
Salt and freshly ground
    black pepper
1 tbsp chopped fresh
    parsley
1 tbsp chopped fresh
    rosemary leaves

For the kebabs
500g thick end of white
    fish like haddock, cod
    or coley
12 button shallots
2 courgettes, cut into
    2.5cm pieces
1 yellow pepper, halved
    and cut into 4cm pieces
3 tomatoes, cut into
    wedges

To serve
1 lemon, cut into wedges
Pitta bread

Mussels in Foil Parcels

500g fresh mussel in their shells per person
1 bunch of spring onions, cut into 2.5cm pieces
2 large beef tomatoes, finely diced
Thick kitchen foil
4 tbsp chopped fresh parsley

To serve
Crusty bread

A very simple and effective way to cook mussels, this gives delicious results. If you go foraging in the rock pools at the seaside when the tide is just going out, you can collect your own mussels – great fun for all the family to do.

- Scrub the mussels well, removing any beards and discarding any that are open and do not close when sharply tapped.

- Make 4 large triple-thickness 35cm squares of foil.

- Divide the cleaned mussels between the four parcel, then sprinkle over the spring onions and tomatoes and top with the parsley. Fold up the edges and seal tightly.

- Cook the mussels over the hot coals for 6–10 minutes according to their size.

- Once cooked, open the parcels carefully and discard any closed mussels.

- Serve hot with crusty bread to mop up the juices in the foil.

CHAPTER 6

Special Occasion Dishes

Large, whole fish, like whole salmon, salmon trout and large trout, are ideal for special occasions. If you don't have a fish kettle, you can hire them from some supermarkets. Alternatively, the fish can be cooked either slightly curled on a deep-sided roasting tin, in a fish poacher or simply wrapped up in treble thickness of heavy-duty foil and cooked in a hot dishwasher – without any detergent, of course!

Thai Smoked Salmon Rolls

12 slices of smoked
  salmon
1 small cucumber, cut
  into matchsticks
1 red chilli, cut in half
  lengthways, de-seeded
  and thinly sliced
2 tbsp chopped fresh
  coriander, mint, basil
  or dill

For the sauce
2 tbsp fresh lime juice
2 tbsp runny honey
2 tbsp sweet chilli sauce
1 tbsp Thai fish sauce

A tasty snack or starter for special occasions,
this looks great but is deceptively simple to
make – as are all the best dishes! The salmon is
bursting with flavour with a hint of the Orient
and is bound to impress your guests.

- Lay out the salmon slices on a large piece
  of clingfilm. Divide the cucumber, chilli
  and herbs evenly between the slices of
  smoked salmon.

- In a bowl, mix all the sauce ingredients
  together and drizzle over the filling, then
  roll each slice tightly into a finger shape.
  Serve chilled.

Stir-fried Crab Claws with Ginger

In many fish markets or supermarkets, especially in Chinese ones, you can buy crab claws already cooked. Don't be fooled by the simplicity of this recipe because the final flavours are superb.

- Preheat a wok or large, heavy-based frying pan and add 1 tbsp of the oil. Add the crab claws and stir-fry for 4–5 minutes. Take out of the wok and keep on a plate.

- Heat the remaining oil, stir in the ginger and cook for 2 minutes.

- Add the spring onions, then return the crab to the wok and add the remaining ingredients. Cover with a lid and cook for 1–2 minutes, then serve immediately.

2 tbsp rapeseed oil
8 brown crab claws, cracked into pieces
50g fresh root ginger, peeled and sliced into fine matchsticks
1 bunch of spring onions, cut into 5cm long strips
2 tbsp soy sauce
Generous pinch of sugar

Savoury Choux Buns with Prawn Filling

65g plain flour
50g butter
150ml water
2 eggs, beaten
Vegetable oil, for deep-
    frying

For the filling
125g soft cream cheese
2 tbsp crème fraîche or
    soured cream
125g shelled small prawns
A squeeze of lemon juice
A little freshly chopped
    parsley

Choux buns are made with a light, crisp pastry used to make cheese aigrettes and other savoury dishes. They are great for snacking on, so ideal for parties or serving to guests before dinner.

- Sift the flour on to a piece of kitchen paper. Put the butter and water into a pan and bring to the boil until the butter has melted.

- Remove from the heat and tip the flour into the water, then beat well with a wooden spoon until combined.

- Return the pan to the heat and beat well over a gentle heat for 1 minute to cook the flour. The mixture will form into a ball.

- Remove from the heat and allow to cool for 1–2 minutes, then gradually beat in the eggs, adding enough to make a piping consistency or a spoonable dough.

- Preheat the oil in a deep-fat fryer or large, heavy-based saucepan to 190°C. Spoon or pipe golf-ball-sized balls of the mixture carefully into the hot oil. Allow to cook for about 6–8 minutes or until risen and golden brown.

- Once cooked, allow to drain on kitchen paper, making a small hole in the side to allow the steam to escape.

- Meanwhile, in a bowl, mix the soft cheese, prawns and crème fraîche together and season to taste with lemon juice, salt and black pepper. Spoon or pipe the prawn mixture into the balls. Garnish with chopped fresh parsley to serve.

Lobster Thermidor

4 x 250g small cooked
  lobsters
100g butter, diced
2 small round shallot,
  very finely chopped
3 tsp chopped fresh
  parsley
4 tsp chopped fresh
  tarragon
8 tbsp dry white wine
600ml Béchamel Sauce
  (page 148)
6 tbsp grated cheese
1 tsp mustard powder
A little ground paprika
  pepper

Although lobsters are rather a luxury, they are wonderful for special occasions, so why not look out for them on special offer and buy one or two to keep in the freezer until you need them to make this impressive dish.

- Cut the lobsters in half lengthwise. Remove the lobster meat from the shells. Discard the dead man's fingers (gills). Chop the claws and meat roughly and cut the tail meat into thick slices.

- Melt half the butter in a pan, add the shallot, parsley and tarragon and fry gently for a few minutes.

- Pour in the wine and simmer for 5 minutes.

- Stir in the béchamel sauce and simmer for a few minutes until it is reduced to a creamy sauce.

- Add the lobster meat to the sauce with half the cheese, the remaining butter and the mustard, salt and a little ground paprika to taste.

- Arrange the mixture in the shells, sprinkle with the remaining cheese and put under a preheated grill for a few minutes until golden brown. Serve at once.

Citrus Dublin Bay Prawns

Dublin Bay prawns are large prawns, so if you can't find them, use langoustines, or the largest prawns you can find, with the shells on. You need to allow about 5–6 prawns for each person. As always, don't overcook.

- Mix together in a bowl the lemon juice, garlic, herbs and butter. Season to taste. Spread the prawns with the butter mixture, cover and leave to chill for 1 hour in the fridge.

- Preheat the grill or barbecue and cook for 4–6 minutes. If preferred, heat a large frying pan and cook the prawns for the same time.

- Serve on hot plates with the lemon and lime wedges and crusty bread to mop up the garlicky juices.

> **To vary**
> Replace the Dublin Bay Prawns with smaller prawns.

Juice of 1 lemon
3 garlic cloves, crushed
6 tbsp chopped fresh
    flatleaf parsley
2 tbsp chopped fresh dill
50g unsalted butter
24 Dublin bay prawns
Salt and freshly ground
    black pepper

To garnish
1 lemon or lime, cut into
    wedges
Warm crusty French bread

Seafood Paella

6 tbsp olive oil
6 chicken drumsticks or
  thighs, with skin on
1 large onion, sliced
1-2 garlic cloves, crushed
4 tomatoes, finely chopped
1 red pepper, deseeded,
  sliced
1 green pepper, deseeded,
  sliced
100g frozen peas
½ ground paprika
450g Arborio rice
A few strands of saffron
900ml strong Fish Stock
  (page 142) or chicken
  stock
500g whole fresh mussels
150g tube squid, sliced
  into 2.5cm pieces
150g peeled prawns
Salt and freshly ground
  black pepper

To serve
1 lemon, sliced
Crusty bread

This classic Spanish dish is perfect for entertaining as it gives you that wow factor that we all look for in recipes to make for special occasions. Assuming you don't have a *paella* – for the recipe is names after the dish it is cooked in – use a wok.

- Heat the oil in a large *paella*, frying pan or wok. Add the chicken and cook for 15–20 minutes or until just cooked. Remove the chicken from the pan and keep it warm.

- Add the onion and garlic to the pan and fry for 3–5 minutes until the onion is just soft.

- Stir in the tomatoes, peppers, peas and paprika pepper. Cook for 5–6 minutes.

- Return the chicken to the pan with the rice, saffron and stock. Bring to the boil, stirring all the time. Reduce the heat and simmer for 20–25 minutes, uncovered, until the stock has been absorbed. Stir frequently during cooking.

- Meanwhile, clean the mussels. Stir the mussels into the rice along with the, squid and prawns. Season well. Serve piping hot with crusty bread and lemon slices.

To vary
Replace the chicken with cubes of firm, skinned and boned white fish or salmon. Add langoustines or a small cooked lobster, or add clams and razor clams to ring the changes.

Coconut Fish Curry

225g potatoes, peeled and
  cut into 2cm pieces
1½ tbsp vegetable oil
1 onion, chopped
2 garlic cloves, chopped
175g aubergine, diced
100ml coconut milk
2 tbsp tikka paste
1 bay leaf
1 red pepper, deseeded,
  sliced
1 tsp curry powder
½ tsp cumin seeds
Large handful baby
  washed spinach
Grated zest and juice of
  1 lemon
1 tbsp chopped fresh
  coriander
Salt and freshly ground
  black pepper
350g firm fish, skinned
  and cut into 2cm pieces
1 tsp red wine vinegar

To garnish
A few sprigs of fresh
  coriander

Ask your fishmonger and for any choice off-cuts for your curry. You will pay a fraction of the price of whole fish or fillets. Serve this recipe with herbed basmati rice and crispy popadoms.

- Bring the potatoes to the boil in salted water, then simmer for 6–8 minutes.

- Heat the oil in a frying pan and gently fry the onion and half the garlic for 3 minutes until beginning to soften.

- Add the aubergine and cook for 6–8 minutes.

- Gently heat the coconut milk with the tikka paste, remaining garlic and bay leaf in a pan for 3–4 minutes.

- Add the pepper, curry powder and cumin, stir well and cook for a further 2–3 minutes. Add the potatoes to the onion mixture with the spinach, lemon zest, 1 tbsp lemon juice and coriander. Season to taste.

- Add the diced fish to the coconut mixture and cook for 5 minutes or until tender. Pour in the vinegar and 2 tsp lemon juice.

- Spoon the fish curry and herby rice on to warmed serving plates and serve garnished with fresh coriander.

Ceviche

The lime juice in the marinade effectively cooks the fish so it doesn't require any further cooking. Do make sure you use very fresh fish for this recipe to get the best results. You can make it with most fish fillets, including mackerel, herring and tilapia.

- Place the fish into a non-metallic bowl.

- In a pestle and mortar, crush the coriander seeds and peppercorns to a fine powder, then mix in the lime juice, chillis and salt and pour over the fish. Cover with clingfilm and chill for 24 hours, turning the fish occasionally.

- Now preheat the oil in a frying pan and gently fry the spring onions for 4–5 minutes.

- Add the tomatoes and pepper sauce to taste and mix together over a high heat for 1–2 minutes. Take off the heat and cool for 30 minutes.

- To serve, drain the fish and discard the marinade. Mix the spring onions, tomatoes and coriander and pour over the fish to serve.

450g fish fillets, skinned and cut diagonally into thin strips
1 tsp coriander seeds
1 tsp black peppercorns
juice of 6 limes
1–2 chilli peppers, deseeded and chopped
1 tsp salt
2 tbsp olive oil
1 bunch of spring onions, sliced
4 tomatoes, chopped
A little pepper or chilli sauce
2 tbsp chopped fresh coriander

Red Snapper in Tangy Dressing

1 lime
2 oranges
1 lemon
10 pink peppercorns,
   coarsely crushed
3–4 tbsp olive oil
2 tsp olive oil
2 tsp rapeseed oil
4 x 175–200g red snapper
   fillets, with skin on,
   rinsed well and patted
   dry
Salt and freshly ground
   black pepper

To serve
Noodles and a green
   vegetable

A refreshing tangy sauce made from limes, lemon and oranges makes this a delicious dish. The pink peppercorns combine with the citrus fruits to give a wonderful flavour that the family will enjoy.

- Preheat the oven to 200°C/gas 6.

- Make the dressing by zesting the citrus fruit very finely into a non-metallic bowl. Squeeze the lemon and stir the juice into the citrus zest. With a sharp stainless steel knife, remove the pith from the fruit and segment the oranges and limes and add to the fruit zest. Add the peppercorns and olive oil and stir well.

- Heat the rapeseed oil in a non-stick pan over a high heat.

- Season the fish with salt and pepper and put into a pan skin-side down. Sear the fillets for 1–2 minutes or until the skin is crisp and golden brown. Carefully turn over into a roasting tin and roast in the oven for 7–9 minutes.

- Put the fillets on a serving dish then cover with the citrus dressing. Serve at once with noodles and a green vegetable.

Whole Roasted Salmon

Whole salmon cooked this way in the oven give such a moist result. It is cooked in its own juices, allowing none of the flavour or goodness to escape and making the flesh very succulent with a lovely flavour.

- Remove and discard the fish bones with tweezers or small pointed pliers.

- In a large pan, heat the oil with the fennel and sauté for about 10 minutes or until soft.

- Oil a large piece of thick gauge foil large enough to go around the salmon twice. Put the foil on to a large baking tray and place the salmon skin-side down on the foil. Top with the fennel, lemon, dill and wine. Season well. Place the other piece of salmon on top skin-side uppermost. Make slashes down the salmon with a sharp knife and brush with a little oil on the skin. Seal the foil round the fish.

- Bake in the oven at 190°C/gas 5 for 30–50 minutes or until the fish is opaque and firm when touched. Do not overcook.

- Serve the salmon hot or cold with seasonal vegetables or salad.

1 x 2.5kg farmed salmon filleted in two halves with skin left on
1 tbsp vegetable oil
1 fennel bulb, trimmed, halved, cored and thinly sliced
1 lemon, thinly sliced
A few sprigs of fresh dill
5 tbsp dry white wine
Salt and freshly ground black pepper

To serve
Seasonal vegetables or salad

Salt-baked Sea Bass

Flaked sea salt
4 x 500g sea bass, scaled

To serve
Tartare Sauce (page 145)
  and lemon wedges

You may not have come across this method
before but it is a great way to cook whole fish
as the results mean the fish is very moist and
tender. You do need to use flaked sea salt for
best results.

- Preheat the oven to 220°C/gas 8.

- Moisten the salt until it sticks together like
  sand. Make sure the salt is firm but not
  runny.

- Put the fish on to a non-metallic baking
  tray. Mould the salt around each fish to a
  depth of 2cm.

- Bake in the oven for about 25–30 minutes.

- To serve, crack open the salt outer casing
  and carefully peel away the salt with the
  skin. Lift out the fish on to a serving plate.

- Serve with tartare sauce and lemon wedges.

> **To vary**
> Replace the flaked sea salt with pink
> Himalayan salt to ring the changes.

CHAPTER 7

Accompaniments

This chapter contains a mixed selection of stock, sauces and accompaniments for fish dishes from Aioli to Melba Toast. Many of them you can buy ready-made in the supermarkets if you prefer, but there is something special about creating a complete meal from scratch, including all the trimmings.

You can use all kinds of herbs when cooking fish, and fresh herbs will give the delicate flavour that works best. Drying concentrates the flavour of herbs, so if you do use dried herbs, use half the quantity. Some herbs you might like to try are curly leaf and flatleaf parsley, fennel, chervil, samphire, dill, tarragon or salad burnet, but there are many more.

Making a fresh herb salt is quick and easy. Pour a little salt into a pestle and mortar with handful of chopped fresh herbs, including the stalks. Grind the salt until it turns green in colour, then rub through a coarse sieve to remove any woody parts of the herbs. Store in an airtight jar for 1 month. Sprinkle the salt over the fish when cooking.

When recipes refer to woody herbs this means herbs like rosemary, bay leaves, sage, etc. Soft herbs are like basil, chervil, parsley, etc.

Fish Stock with Herbs

1kg fish bones, tails,
  skin and fish heads
1.2l cold water
500ml dry white wine
  (optional)
1 onion or 2 banana
  shallots, finely chopped
1 leek, cleaned and sliced
2 carrots, sliced
10 parsley stalks
1–2 bay leaves
6 black peppercorns

The secret to making a good fish stock is not to allow it to boil otherwise it will go cloudy, so keep your stock at barely a simmer – the surface should just be shimmering. A fish stock does need to be well seasoned.

- Wash any blood away from the bones and especially the gills otherwise the stock will be cloudy.

- Put the fish trimmings, water and wine into a large saucepan over a gentle heat and very slowly bring to a simmer.

- Skim the surface of the stock to remove the grey scum and discard it.

- When the scum has stopped rising to the top of the pan, add the remaining ingredients. Simmer for about 30 minutes, removing any scum when necessary.

- Strain the stock and discard the fish and vegetables.

- Leave to cool, then store in the fridge for no more than 2 days.

- To reheat the stock, bring it to a rolling boil, then boil to reduce a little.

- If you like, you can reduce the stock by one-third, then and freeze in ice cube bags for 4–6 months.

To vary
To make a shellfish bisque, use the shells of prawns, mussels, crab and lobster, broken into pieces, in place of the fish heads and bones.

Simple Fish Stock

Fish bones
Water
1 leek, sliced
1 onion, chopped
1 celery stick, chopped
6 black peppercorns
100ml white wine

If you eat fish regularly, you will inevitably have bones to get rid of, and what better way to make use of them than to make a white fish stock. Always make sure you clean off any blood before you start.

- Wash the fish bones to remove any blood, then chop them into pieces to fit into the pot. Add enough cold water to cover.

- Add the leeks, onion, celery, peppercorns and half the wine, bring slowly to a simmer, then simmer for 20 minutes.

- Strain the stock into a clean pan and simmer the stock gently, without allowing it to boil, until it is reduced by half.

- Season to taste, then freeze the stock in ice cube bags.

Mayonnaise

You can quickly make your own mayonnaise in a food processor or blender, which takes the hard work out of whisking while you slowly add the oil. Make sure the egg yolks are at room temperature for best results.

2 large egg yolks
2 tbsp wine vinegar or
   fresh lemon juice
300ml oil
Salt and freshly ground
   black pepper
Pinch of sugar
1 tsp ready-made mustard

- Turn on a food processor or blender and drop in the large egg yolks and 1 tbsp of the vinegar or fresh lemon juice and blend well.

- With the processor running as slowly as possible, gradually pour in 300ml oil. Add the remaining wine vinegar and season with salt, pepper and a pinch of sugar. Add a little mustard to taste. The mixture should be thick.

- The mayonnaise will keep for 3 days in a sealed box in the fridge.

Flavoured mayonnaise
To make a flavoured mayonnaise, add one of the following:

- 2–4 tsp chopped and drained capers;
- 1 tbsp chopped fresh herbs like tarragon, chives, parsley;
- 2–3 puréed sun-dried tomatoes;
- 2–3 tbsp finely chopped cucumber;
- 2 tbsp curry paste.

Aioli

4 plump garlic cloves,
   skinned
a little salt, about ¼ ml
   spoon
2 egg yolks
300ml light or virgin olive
   oil
30 ml fresh lemon juice

Aioli is a garlic mayonnaise, which is a good sauce to serve with fish, raw crudités and cooked vegetables.

- In a large bowl, crush the garlic with the salt, then beat until a smooth paste is formed.

- Beat in the egg yolks.

- Gradually pour in the oil a little at a time, whisking continuously until the mixture thickens.

- Beat in the lemon juice.

- Keep for up to 3 days chilled in the fridge.

Cook's tip
Ideally use fresh garlic.

Tartare Sauce

This is the classic cold sauce for fish, especially for fish fried in batter or cooked in breadcrumbs.

- Mix all the ingredients together, cover and leave in the fridge for 2 hours before use.

To vary
Omit the herbs and replace them with 1–1½ tsp anchovy essence.

150ml Mayonnaise
(page 143)
1 tsp chopped fresh
tarragon or parsley
2 tsp capers, drained and
finely chopped
2 tsp finely chopped
gherkin
1 tbsp lemon or lime
juice

French Dressing

1 tsp Dijon mustard
Pinch of sugar
1 tbsp vinegar
Salt and freshly ground
    black pepper
6 tbsp olive oil

A simple way to make French Dressing is to put all the ingredients into a screw-topped jar, make sure the lid is on securely and shake well.

● Whisk the mustard, sugar, vinegar, salt and pepper.

● Gradually whisk in the oil until all the ingredients are completely amalgamated and thickened.

Pesto Sauce

This classic Italian sauce goes so well with fish dishes. You can buy ready-made but it is easy and satisfying to make your own.

- Put the wild garlic, basil or rocket in a food processor or pestle and mortar, and process or pound well to form a paste.

- Slowly blend in the garlic cloves, pine nuts, freshly grated Parmesan cheese and olive oil.

- Store in a screw-topped jar in the fridge for up to a week.

> **To vary**
> Replace the pine nuts with other shelled nuts like ground almonds, finely chopped walnuts, pecans, etc.

MAKES ABOUT 200ML

50g wild garlic, basil or rocket
2–3 garlic cloves, peeled
20–40g pine nuts
50g Parmesan cheese, freshly grated
100ml olive oil

Béchamel Sauce

450ml milk
A few sprigs of fresh
 parsley
1 bay leaf
1 blade of mace or a
 pinch of ground mace
 (optional)
10 whole black
 peppercorns
1 slice onion, 5mm thick
40g butter
20g plain flour
Salt and freshly ground
 black pepper

Béchamel is the classic white sauce that you can use for all kinds of dishes, either as a simple white sauce, or flavoured with herbs – notably for parsley sauce – cheese or other ingredients.

- Pour the milk in a small saucepan and add the parsley, bay leaf, mace (if using), peppercorns and onion. Place over a low heat for about 5 minutes until it comes slowly to a simmer.

- Remove from the heat and leave to cool, then strain the milk into a jug, discarding the flavourings.

- Melt the butter over a low heat, then whisk in the flour to make a shiny paste. Gradually add the milk, whisking all the time, until you have a smooth and glossy sauce.

- Turn the heat to minimum and cook for 5 minutes, whisking occasionally.

Home-made Tomato Sauce

You can use this sauce on its own or as the basis for many other sauces not only for fish, but also for meat and vegetables.

- Fry the onion and bacon with the butter for 5 minutes.

- Stir in the flour, then pour in the tomatoes and herbs and season with salt and pepper. Simmer gently for 15 minutes.

- Rub the sauce through a sieve into a clean pan with the back of a wooden spoon, then re-season to taste. Simmer to reduce the sauce until it is the consistency you prefer.

½ onion, chopped
2 rashers bacon, rinded and finely chopped
15g butter
15g plain flour
400g can tomatoes
2 tsp fresh mixed herbs
Salt and freshly ground black pepper

> **To vary**
> You can add 2 chopped garlic cloves when frying the onion and bacon. For a smooth sauce, blend the sauce in a food processor then sieve well.

Hollandaise Sauce

2 tbsp white wine or
    tarragon vinegar
1 tbsp water
2 large egg yolks
225g unsalted butter,
    softened
Salt and freshly ground
    white pepper

This is a classic sauce, light and delicate, that is perfect to serve with fish – as well as chicken and vegetables like asparagus. It is a little prone to curdling so work slowly and carefully and you will create a delicious, smooth sauce.

- Put the wine vinegar and water in a pan, bring to the boil, then simmer until the liquid has reduced by half. Put to one side to cool.

- Pour the reduced vinegar and the eggs into a heatproof bowl set over a pan of simmering water. Whisk the mixture until it becomes thick and fluffy.

- Gradually add the butter a small piece at a time, whisking briskly, until the sauce become the consistency of mayonnaise. Season to taste.

- Keep warm in a vacuum flask until ready to serve.

To vary
You can use the juice of a fresh lemon instead of the wine vinegar if you prefer.

Mousseline Sauce

This is a richer version of Hollandaise Sauce, made by adding 45ml of lightly whipped cream to your hollandaise just before serving.
To vary, replace the vinegar or lemon juice with blood oranges.

Mushy Peas

A great accompaniment for fish and chips.

1 bag frozen peas
Salt

- Cook the frozen peas as directed on the packet.
- Drain well and blend in a processor until just coarsely mashed.
- Stir in seasoning and add a little cream if liked.

Chunky Chips

900g large potatoes
Salt
Vegetable oil like
    rapeseed

Not something you should indulge in every day, but when you fancy some chips, nothing else will do, so here's a traditional recipe, or you can use the healthier version that follows.

- Peel the potatoes and cut into thick slices, then into chips. Leave in a bowl of cold water for 30 minutes until the starch is removed. Drain well and pat dry.
- Heat a heavy-based pan or deep-fat fryer only one-third full to 190°C or until one chip dropped in the hot oil rises to the surface.
- Quarter-fill the frying basket, lower into the oil carefully and cook for 6–7 minutes or until the chips just start to get a golden colour.
- Carefully raise the basket from the pan, allowing the temperature to rise back up to 190°C. Fry all the chips for a second time for a further 3–4 minutes until crispy and golden brown. Drain well on kitchen paper.

Healthier Chips

SERVES 4

For this version, you par-boil the chips, then roast them in a little oil in a hot oven so you get delicious results – crunchy outside and soft inside – without double deep-fat frying.

900g large potatoes,
  such as Desiree
2–3 tbsp light oil olive
Salt

- Peel the potatoes or leave the skin on and scrub well, as you prefer. Cut into thick slices, then into chips.

- Bring a pan of water to the boil. Add the chips and cook for 2 minutes. Drain well and then pat dry with kitchen paper.

- Preheat the oven to 240°C/gas 8.

- Tip the blanched potatoes into a large non-stick roasting tin, sprinkle with the oil, toss the chips in the oil and season with salt

- Roast in the oven for 40 minutes or until golden brown and cooked, turning occasionally.

- Drain on kitchen paper before serving with salt to taste.

Melba Toast

4 slices white or brown
bread

This thin, crisp toast is the perfect
accompaniment for pâté and other light starters.
It is so easy to make your own, that it is hardly
worth buying.

- Preheat the grill to high and toast the
  bread lightly on both sides.

- Cut off the crusts then, holding the toast
  flat, slide the knife between the toasted
  edges to split the bread in halve
  lengthways. Cut each square into triangles,
  then toast the untoasted side uppermost
  under the grill until the untoasted surface
  starts to curl and turn golden brown.

- Serve warm.

Home-made Breadcrumbs

You can make your own fresh breadcrumbs or, if the recipe calls for dried breadcrumbs, simply dry them out in the oven.

Use white or brown bread at least a day old

- Cut the crusts off the bread if you prefer white breadcrumbs.

- If you are using a food processor, simply turn on the rotating blades, drop large pieces of bread on to the blades and process until the crumbs are fine enough.

- If you do not have a processor, simply use a grater.

- If dry breadcrumbs are required, place the fresh crumbs on a baking tray and allow them to dry out in the oven on a very low heat, 140°C/gas 1, stirring occasionally to prevent uneven colouring.

- Store dried breadcrumbs in an airtight jar.

Garlic Croûtons

4 slices of bread, cut into
  small squares
100ml olive oil
1 garlic clove, chopped

So useful to sprinkle on soups or salads to add flavour and crunch, just leave out the garlic to make plain croûtons, although it does add interest and piquancy. You can also use toasted bread if you prefer.

- Heat the oil in a pan with the garlic.

- Add the bread squares and toss lightly in the oil until crisp and golden, then lift them out of the pan with a slotted spoon and drain on kitchen paper.

To vary
Omit the garlic if you prefer.

Index

SOME OTHER TITLES FROM HOW TO BOOKS

THE HEALTHY LIFESTYLE DIET COOKBOOK
SARAH FLOWER

Tired of fad diets and yo-yo dieting? Do you want to lose weight and improve your health but still enjoy your food? Nutritionist Sarah Flower believes that by following the recipes in her book you can eat well, lose weight, feel better AND stay that way. Sarah's focus is on healthy eating and delicious food that all the family will enjoy. She also describes lifestyle changes that everyone can adopt to lay the foundations for healthy eating and to lose unwanted pounds if they need to. Sarah also includes superfoods, menu plans and some food swap suggestions.

ISBN 978-1-905862-74-0

MAKE YOUR OWN JELLIED PRESERVES
An easy guide to home and hedgerow jelly making
CAROLINE PAKENHAM

This book will show you how you can use the fruits and herbs you can grow in your garden, or the fruits that you can pick yourself from the hedgerows, to make into jars of delicious jelly preserves – quickly, easily, cheaply, and without fuss. It will enable even the true beginner to understand what to do, and feel confident and proud of their end product. The book includes full colour photos to help you recognise hedgerow fruits, plus numerous recipes for fruits that you can gather locally from spring to autumn or buy from further afield.

ISBN 978-1-905862-76-4

EAT WELL, SPEND LESS
The complete money-saving guide to everyday cooking
SARAH FLOWER

This invaluable book contains over 200 great family recipes for busy cooks who want to save time and money, but also deliver wholesome food for their families. It's also an essential housekeeper's guide for the 21st century. Nutritionist Sarah Flower shows you how to feed yourself and your family a healthy balanced diet without spending hours in the kitchen and a fortune in the supermarket.

ISBN 978-1-905862-83-2

EVERYDAY THAI COOKING
Easy, authentic recipes from Thailand to cook at home for friends and family
SIRIPAN AKVANICH

Everyday Thai Cooking brings you the secrets of cooking delicious Thai food straight from Thailand. Author Siripan Akvanich draws on her years of experience of cooking for her restaurant customers in Thailand to enable you to create authentic Thai dishes, ranging from curries and meat and fish dishes to wonderful Thai desserts. With clear instructions and insider tips, Siripan helps you bring these dishes – many of them traditional family recipes – to life and shows you how to make them *a-roi* (delicious)!

ISBN 978-1-905862-85-6

EVERYDAY COOKING FOR ONE
Imaginative, delicious and healthy recipes that make cooking for one fun
WENDY HOBSON

Here is a collection of simple, tasty meals specially designed for one that can help you enjoy your everyday eating. Starting with sensible tips for shopping and for stocking your food cupboard, you'll find recipes for everything from snacks to delicious fish; and meat and vegetable main courses that keep an eye on a healthy dietary balance and a healthy bank balance. And there's a unique feature, too. Some recipes just don't work in small quantities, and that could include some of your favourites. So we've included some of those recipes like casseroles, roasts and cakes and shown you how to create four different meals from one single cooking session.

ISBN 978-1-905862-94-8

How To Books are available through all good bookshops, or you can order direct from us through Grantham Book Services.

Tel: +44 (0)1476 541080
Fax: +44 (0)1476 541061
Email: orders@gbs.tbs-ltd.co.uk

Or via our website
www.howtobooks.co.uk

To order via any of these methods please quote the title(s) of the book(s) and your credit card number together with its expiry date.

For further information about our books and catalogue, please contact:

How To Books
Spring Hill House
Spring Hill Road
Begbroke
Oxford
OX5 1RX

Visit our web site at
www.howtobooks.co.uk

Or you can contact us by email at info@howtobooks.co.uk